COOKING WITH

Bon Appétit

COOKING WITH

Bon Appétit

Recipe
Yearbook
1992

Editors' Choice of Recipes from 1991

THE KNAPP PRESS
Publishers
Los Angeles

Copyright © 1992 by Knapp Communications Corporation

Published by The Knapp Press
5900 Wilshire Boulevard, Los Angeles, California 90036

Library of Congress Catalog Number: 89-650935

ISBN: 0-89535-998-7

On the Cover: *German Lebkuchen Cake with White Chocolate Frosting, English Chocolate Trifle with Apricots and Raspberries, and Brazilian Banana and White Chocolate Ice Cream Torte.*
Photographed by Lannen/Kelly.

Printed and bound in the United States of America
10   9   8   7   6   5   4   3   2   1

❧ Contents

❦ Foreword

Imagine taking all twelve 1991 issues of *Bon Appétit* and going to each of the very particular editors on the magazine's staff and asking them for their favorite recipes from the thousands we published over the year; then asking them to select the recipes they think best represent the most interesting trends and culinary developments that transpired during the past 12 months; and then taking all those recommendations, adding a review of the year's hottest products, places and people, and compiling everything in one easy-to-read, lovely-to-look-at place. That's exactly what we did, and the result is this, our sixth annual *Bon Appétit* yearbook, with more than 175 utterly delicious recipes for everything from appetizers to desserts.

One thing the magazine's editors are *not* particular about is the style or formality of a recipe: Good food is good food whether the recipe was created by a superstar chef or simply one of our readers. As a result, you'll find that the recipes included here run the gamut from restaurant-style sophisticated to down-home simple, from elegant dinner-party fare to dishes ideal for midweek family suppers. What's here is a lot like what you'll find in the magazine itself: something for everyone. That's because we've culled our selections from every area of *Bon Appétit*, including always-popular departments like "Cooking Healthy" and "Too Busy to Cook?" as well as entertaining, cooking class and restaurant features.

The variety of recipes featured in *Bon Appétit* is represented here in two ways: in the many types of dishes offered, everything from soups, salads, pastas and pizzas to side dishes, breads and super desserts, and in the number of different cuisines featured, including French, Italian, Mexican, Chinese, Swiss, English, good old southern American, southwestern, New England-style, even Indonesian. The variety is apparent throughout the book and within each chapter, meaning you'll come across the likes of Creamy Polenta with Sage and Roasted Wild Mushrooms as well as Jalapeño Cheese Squares in the "Appetizers" section.

In the past few years, Americans seem to have really taken to heart (pun intended) the idea of eating right and cooking light for longer, healthier lives. The call for streamlined recipes is answered throughout this yearbook, as in Grilled Pompano with Spinach and Cherry Tomatoes or Mixed-Grain and Vegetable Stir-Fry, plus an entire page of "Diet News" is included in the section at the back of the book. In addition to health-conscious recipes, Americans also want quick-cooking, simple recipes for those times—probably most every night of the work week, if you're like a lot of people—when there just isn't time to cook. Look for easy-to-make dishes in every chapter, from the Spiced Mixed Nuts in "Appetizers" to Skirt Steak with Shallots in "Main Courses" to the Apple and Raisin Crisp in "Desserts."

And since *Bon Appétit* is as much about the world of food as it is about recipes, we've concluded our yearbook with a section called "News '91—The Year of Food and Entertaining in Review." It includes some of the year's best new products and interesting trends, foods you can order by mail, favorite books, the latest on the hottest restaurants and getaways, plus a wish list of things you'll want to have for the well-outfitted kitchen and table. (All the prices, addresses and other details have been updated as of this book's publication date.)

We hope you enjoy this culinary year in review as much as we did then—and now.

1 ❦ Appetizers

Appetizers are a lot like desserts: You don't really need one to make a meal complete (though all you chocoholics out there would probably argue that statement), but they really dress up a menu. So when we do go all out, preparing savory appetizers and sumptuous desserts, it's likely we're entertaining, since that's when we have the time and inclination to prepare that little something extra. Of course entertaining these days can mean a sophisticated, sit-down dinner party, a backyard barbecue, an afternoon get-together in front of the tube, a leisurely weekend morning brunch—anything you want it to, basically. And that's why there is a wide selection of appetizers here, something to suit the occasion, wherever and whatever it might be.

For that intimate, late-night dinner, consider Boudin Blanc Terrine with Red Onion Confit, an elegant, pretty first course that can be prepared three days ahead. If you like the idea of chips and dip for something casual but don't want to prepare the same old thing, try Black-eyed Pea Dip, a new version of the classic bean dip.

Appetizers can start a party on just the right note; they can also be the stars of the party if it's a cocktails-and-finger-food occasion, which is always a great way to entertain. The Jalapeño Cheese Squares and Smoked Salmon Spirals here would fit right in at this type of event.

Boudin Blanc Terrine with Red Onion Confit

The terrine is made with the same ingredients used in boudin blanc, *the classic French white sausage. Start preparation at least two days before serving.*

8 servings

1½ cups whipping cream
2 medium onions, chopped
5 teaspoons salt
3 bay leaves
3 whole cloves
1 large garlic clove, crushed
1 teaspoon pepper
⅛ teaspoon ground nutmeg
  Pinch of dried thyme, crumbled
8 large shallots, minced

1 tablespoon butter
1 pound trimmed boneless center pork loin, sinew removed, cut into 1-inch chunks, well chilled

3 eggs
6 tablespoons all purpose flour
¼ cup tawny Port
3 tablespoons dried currants, minced

Lettuce leaves
Cracked peppercorns
Minced fresh parsley
Bay leaves
Red Onion Confit (see recipe)
French bread baguette slices

Combine first 9 ingredients in heavy medium saucepan. Add 3 minced shallots. Bring to simmer. Remove from heat, cover and let stand 30 minutes. Refrigerate cream mixture overnight.

Preheat oven to 325°F. Line 7-cup pâté or bread pan with plastic wrap. Melt butter in heavy small skillet over low heat. Add remaining 5 shallots. Cover and cook until very soft, stirring occasionally, about 15 minutes. Transfer to processor. Add pork, eggs flour and Port and puree until smooth. Strain cream mixture, pressing on solids to extract as much liquid as possible. With processor running, add cream through feed tube and process just until cream is combined with pork. Transfer to large bowl. Mix in currants.

Spoon pork mixture into prepared pan. Cover with foil. Place pan in larger pan. Add boiling water to larger pan to within ½ inch of top of terrine. Bake until terrine begins to shrink from sides of pan and knife inserted into center comes out clean, about 1½ hours. Uncover and cool on rack. Refrigerate until well chilled. (*Can be prepared 3 days ahead. Cover and keep refrigerated.*)

Line platter with lettuce leaves. Arrange terrine atop leaves. Sprinkle pepper and parsley over terrine. Garnish with bay leaves. Spoon confit around sides. Serve with French bread baguette slices.

Red Onion Confit

You might also try this condiment alongside roast poultry and meat or in sandwiches and omelets.

8 servings

3 tablespoons olive oil
2 large red onions (about 1½ pounds), halved, sliced
3 tablespoons dried currants
3 tablespoons red wine vinegar

1 tablespoon canned chicken broth
2 teaspoons chopped fresh thyme or ¾ teaspoon dried, crumbled
½ teaspoon sugar

Heat oil in heavy large skillet over medium-high heat. Add onions and sauté until crisp-tender, about 8 minutes. Add all remaining ingredients and stir until liquid is reduced to thick glaze, about 4 minutes. Season to taste with salt and pepper. (*Can be prepared 2 days ahead. Cover with plastic and refrigerate.*) Serve confit warm or at room temperature.

Creamy Polenta with Sage and Roasted Wild Mushrooms

Contrasting textures and Italian flavors star in this appetizer.

4 servings

Polenta
1¾ cups (or more) water
1¾ cups chicken stock or canned broth
1 teaspoon minced garlic
¾ cup polenta (Italian cornmeal) or cornmeal

Sage
½ cup olive oil or peanut oil
⅓ cup fresh sage leaves

⅔ cup crème fraîche* or sour cream
¼ cup grated Monterey Jack cheese
¼ cup grated Parmesan cheese
3 tablespoons butter
Roasted Wild Mushrooms (see recipe)

For polenta: Preheat oven to 350°F. Bring 1¾ cups water, chicken stock and minced garlic to boil in heavy large ovenproof saucepan over medium-high heat. Gradually stir in polenta. Reduce heat to medium and cook 5 minutes, stirring constantly. Cover and transfer to oven. Bake until thick but still creamy (add more water if mixture appears dry), stirring occasionally, about 45 minutes.

Meanwhile, prepare sage: Heat olive oil in heavy small skillet to 375°F. Fry fresh sage leaves in batches until crisp, about 10 seconds. Using slotted spoon, transfer to paper towels and drain. Season with salt.

Remove polenta from oven. Stir in crème fraîche, grated Monterey Jack cheese, grated Parmesan cheese and butter. Season generously with salt and pepper. Spoon polenta on plates. Top with Roasted Wild Mushrooms. Garnish with fried sage and serve immediately.

*Crème fraîche is available at specialty foods stores and some supermarkets. If unavailable, heat 1 cup whipping cream to lukewarm (85°F). Remove whipping cream from heat and mix in 2 tablespoons buttermilk. Cover and let stand in warm draft-free area until slightly thickened, 24 to 48 hours, depending on temperature of room. Chill until ready to use.

Roasted Wild Mushrooms

Delicious alongside roasted meats as well as atop the creamy polenta.

4 servings

8 garlic cloves, thinly sliced
3 tablespoons olive oil
3 tablespoons balsamic vinegar or red wine vinegar
3 fresh rosemary sprigs or 1 teaspoon dried, crumbled

3 fresh thyme sprigs or 1 teaspoon dried, crumbled
4 cups large fresh wild mushrooms (such as shiitake, oyster or cremini)

Preheat oven to 425°F. Line 2 baking sheets with foil. Combine sliced garlic, olive oil, balsamic vinegar, rosemary and thyme in bowl. Add mushrooms and toss to coat. Season with salt and pepper. Arrange in single layer on prepared baking sheets. Roast until mushrooms are tender and slightly crisp on edges, about 25 minutes. Serve immediately.

Spiced Mixed Nuts

Makes about 2½ cups

2½ cups mixed whole almonds, raw cashews, pecans and/or raw peanuts
2 tablespoons vegetable oil

2 teaspoons chili powder
¼ to ½ teaspoon cayenne pepper
2 tablespoons sugar
1 teaspoon salt

Preheat oven to 300°F. Place mixed nuts in large bowl. Heat vegetable oil in heavy small saucepan over medium heat. Add chili powder and cayenne pepper to taste and stir until aromatic, about 15 seconds. Pour over mixed nuts. Add sugar and salt and stir to blend. Transfer to baking pan. Bake until mixed nuts are toasted, stirring occasionally, about 20 minutes. Serve warm or at room temperature. (*Can be made 5 days ahead. Cover and store at room temperature.*)

Roasted Bell Peppers with Basil and Balsamic Vinegar

This easy starter is delicious served with Italian bread.

8 servings

3 red bell peppers
3 yellow bell peppers
4½ tablespoons olive oil
1½ tablespoons balsamic vinegar or red wine vinegar

1 tablespoon matchstick-size orange peel strips (orange part only)
12 large fresh basil leaves

Char bell peppers over gas flame or in broiler until blackened on all sides. Wrap in paper bag and let stand at least 10 minutes. Peel and seed. Rinse if necessary; pat dry. Cut into ¾-inch-wide strips. Place in bowl. Mix in oil, vinegar and orange peel. Season with salt and pepper. Let stand 1 hour. (*Can be prepared 1 day ahead. Cover and refrigerate. Bring to room temperature before serving.*) Chop basil; mix into peppers and serve.

Pecan-Cheese Spread

6 servings

4 bacon slices
¾ cup pecan pieces

2 cups firmly packed grated cheddar cheese
4 ounces cream cheese, room temperature

2 tablespoons mayonnaise
⅛ teaspoon hot pepper sauce (such as Tabasco)
⅛ teaspoon Worcestershire sauce
3 green onions, sliced
Crackers

Fry bacon in heavy large skillet over medium heat until crisp. Transfer to paper towel to cool. Add pecans to drippings and cook until golden brown, stirring occasionally, about 5 minutes. Transfer to paper towel to cool. Season with salt.

Blend cheddar, cream cheese, mayonnaise, hot pepper sauce and Worcestershire sauce in processor until smooth. Transfer to bowl and stir in green onions. Crumble bacon and add to mixture. Line cookie sheet with plastic. Drop mixture by spoonfuls onto plastic, forming 8-inch strip. Freeze 20 minutes to firm slightly. Using plastic as aid, form log shape. Remove plastic; roll log in pecans to coat. Wrap and refrigerate until firm. (*Can be prepared 1 week ahead.*) Serve cheese spread with crackers.

Crabmeat Cheesecakes with Crab Sauce

4 servings

Sauce

1 2½-pound cooked crab

4 cups water
1 cup dry white wine
1 onion, chopped
2 carrots, chopped
1 garlic clove, minced
2 tablespoons tomato paste
1 bouquet garni (3 parsley sprigs,
    3 thyme sprigs, 1 bay leaf,
    10 peppercorns, tied up in
    cheesecloth)
½ cup whipping cream

Cheesecakes

6 ounces cream cheese, room
    temperature
2 large eggs
½ shallot, minced
1 tablespoon chopped seeded
    tomato
1 small garlic clove
1½ teaspoons minced fresh dill
1½ teaspoons fresh lemon juice
    Cayenne pepper

½ cup (1 stick) chilled unsalted
    butter, cut into pieces
    Caviar (optional)

For sauce: Preheat oven to 350°F. Crack crab and remove meat from shells; cover and chill meat until ready to use. Place crab shells in roasting pan. Roast until aromatic, about 20 minutes.

Transfer shells to heavy large saucepan. Mix in water, wine, onion, carrots, garlic, tomato paste and bouquet garni and bring to boil. Reduce heat and simmer until liquid is reduced to ½ cup, stirring occasionally, about 1½ hours. Strain. Add cream to cooking liquid and simmer until reduced to ¾ cup, stirring occasionally, about 10 minutes. (*Sauce can be prepared to this point up to 1 day ahead. Cover and refrigerate.*)

For cheesecakes: Butter four ⅔-cup soufflé dishes. Using electric mixer, beat cream cheese in medium bowl until fluffy. Beat in eggs. Mix in shallot, tomato, garlic, dill and lemon juice. Stir in crabmeat. Season to taste with salt, pepper and cayenne. Divide mixture among dishes. Bake until centers are set, about 30 minutes. Cool cheesecakes slightly.

Run sharp knife around sides of cups to loosen cheesecakes. Turn 1 out onto each plate. Bring sauce to simmer. Gradually add butter and whisk until melted. Season to taste with salt, pepper and cayenne. Spoon sauce over cheese-cakes. Garnish with caviar if desired.

Curried Mussels

A sophisticated first course.

4 servings

2 cups dry white wine
1 tablespoon curry powder
2 garlic cloves, minced
1 bay leaf
2 pounds mussels, scrubbed,
    debearded

2 cups whipping cream
1 celery stalk, diced
1 leek, diced
1 carrot, diced
½ medium onion, diced
1 tablespoon fresh lemon juice

Bring first 4 ingredients to simmer in heavy large saucepan over medium-high heat. Add mussels and cover. Cook until mussels open, about 5 minutes. Transfer mussels to serving bowls using slotted spoon; discard any that do not open. Cover and keep warm. Add cream, celery, leek, carrot and onion to cooking liquid. Simmer until vegetables are tender, about 15 minutes. Stir in lemon juice. Season to taste with salt and pepper. Spoon sauce over mussels.

Avocado and Mozzarella with Vinaigrette

8 servings

½ cup olive oil
3 tablespoons red wine vinegar
1 garlic clove, minced
3 ripe avocados, halved, pitted, peeled, cubed

15 ounces (about) fresh mozzarella cheese in water,* drained, cubed
¼ cup chopped fresh basil

Whisk first 3 ingredients in large bowl to blend. Add avocados, mozzarella and basil and toss. Season with salt and pepper.

*Available at specialty foods stores and some supermarkets.

Black-eyed Pea Dip

A new variation of the classic bean dip.

6 servings

1¼ cups dried black-eyed peas
2 garlic cloves, sliced

1 3-ounce package cream cheese, room temperature
1 teaspoon cayenne pepper
1 teaspoon chili powder

1½ cups shredded cheddar cheese (about 6 ounces)
1 bunch green onions, sliced
Tortilla chips

Place peas in heavy medium saucepan. Add enough water to saucepan to cover peas by 2 inches. Let stand 30 minutes. Drain. Add water to cover peas by 2 inches. Generously salt water. Stir in 1 garlic clove. Boil until peas are very tender, adding more water to pan if necessary, about 1 hour.

Using slotted spoon, transfer peas to processor. Process until smooth. Add remaining garlic clove and next 3 ingredients. Pulse until smooth. Season to taste with salt and pepper. Transfer dip to 8-inch-diameter pie plate or quiche dish. (*Can be prepared 2 days ahead. Cover and refrigerate.*)

Preheat oven to 400°F. Top dip with cheddar. Bake until dip is heated through and cheese bubbles, about 20 minutes. Sprinkle dip with green onions and serve with tortilla chips.

Smoked Salmon Spirals

12 servings

1 daikon (Japanese white radish),* peeled

4 ounces cream cheese, room temperature
1 tablespoon fresh dill, finely chopped, or 1 teaspoon dried dillweed
1 tablespoon finely chopped fresh Italian parsley

2 teaspoons drained capers
1½ teaspoons Dijon mustard
½ teaspoon grated lemon peel
⅛ teaspoon cracked pepper
4 ounces sliced smoked salmon, cut into 1-inch-wide strips
Cucumber slices
Fresh dill sprigs
Lemon slices

Using vegetable peeler, cut off thin 8 × 1-inch strips down length of daikon.

Mix cream cheese, dill, parsley, capers, mustard, lemon peel and pepper in small bowl. Spread about 1½ teaspoons mixture on 1 side of each radish strip. Top with salmon. Roll up tightly. Arrange spiral side up on platter. Garnish with cucumber, dill sprigs and lemon.

*Daikon radishes are available at oriental markets and some supermarkets.

Avocado Filled with Marinated Scallops and Mussels

A beautiful and tasty appetizer, light lunch or supper. Serve with crusty bread. Begin preparing recipe one day ahead.

6 servings

Mayonnaise
  - 1 egg yolk
  - 2 tablespoons white wine vinegar
  - 1 tablespoon Dijon mustard
  - 1 garlic clove
  - ½ teaspoon salt
  - ½ teaspoon Worcestershire sauce
  - ¼ teaspoon pepper
    Dash of hot pepper sauce (such as Tabasco)
  - 1 cup vegetable oil

  - ½ cup dry white wine
  - 1½ cups water
  - 1 pound mussels, scrubbed, debearded

  - ¼ cup fresh lemon juice
  - 1 pound bay scallops

  - 3 medium avocados, halved, peeled
  - 2 tablespoons fresh lemon juice
    Curly lettuce leaves
    Minced fresh parsley

For mayonnaise: Combine first 8 ingredients in processor. Process 1 minute. With machine running, gradually add oil in thin steady stream. Continue processing until mixture is thick. (*Mayonnaise can be prepared up to 3 days ahead. Cover and refrigerate.*)

Bring wine and ½ cup water to boil in large saucepan over medium-high heat. Add mussels, cover and cook until mussels just open, about 4 minutes. Cool slightly. Carefully remove mussels from shells. Discard shells and any unopened mussels. Chill mussels.

Combine remaining 1 cup water, ¼ cup lemon juice and scallops in medium saucepan. Bring to boil. Remove from heat. Cover and refrigerate scallops until well chilled. Drain thoroughly.

Combine mussels and scallops in bowl. Stir in ¾ cup mayonnaise. Cover and refrigerate at least 12 hours. (*Can be prepared 1 day ahead.*)

Rub avocado halves with 2 tablespoons lemon juice to prevent discoloration. Line 6 plates with lettuce leaves. Place avocado half, cut side up, on each. Spoon scallop mixture into avocados, mounding slightly in center. Or slice avocados, fanning slices atop lettuce; divide scallop mixture among plates. Sprinkle with parsley and serve.

Jalapeño Cheese Squares

A simple appetizer perfect for a crowd.

Makes about 72 squares

  - 10 large eggs
  - ¼ cup minced fresh jalapeño chilies
  - 2 tablespoons chili powder
  - 4 teaspoons ground cumin
  - 1½ cups milk (do not use lowfat or nonfat)

  - 4 cups grated Monterey Jack cheese (about 1 pound)
  - 2 cups chopped green onions (about 12)
  - 4 cups grated cheddar cheese (about 1 pound)

Preheat oven to 350°F. Butter two 9-inch square glass baking dishes. Whisk first 4 ingredients in large bowl to blend. Whisk in milk. Add Monterey Jack cheese and onions and stir to combine. Divide mixture between prepared dishes. Sprinkle half of cheddar cheese over each dish. Bake until tops are light brown and puffed, about 45 minutes. Cool slightly. Cut into 1½-inch squares. (*Can be prepared 8 hours ahead. Transfer squares to heavy large cookie sheet. Cover and refrigerate. Before serving, rewarm in 350°F oven until heated through, about 10 minutes.*) Transfer cheese squares to platter and serve.

Garlicky Eggplant Spread

8 servings

2 large eggplants
(about 2½ pounds)
2 large garlic cloves, slivered

¼ cup olive oil
2 tablespoons fresh lemon juice
2 tablespoons chopped fresh
oregano or 2 teaspoons dried,
crumbled
1 teaspoon ground cumin

Red leaf lettuce
4 tomatoes, sliced
Pita bread
Chopped fresh oregano

Preheat oven to 450°F. Cut slits in eggplants with tip of knife and insert garlic sliver into each slit. Place eggplants in baking pan and bake until very tender, about 1 hour. Cut each eggplant in half and cool slightly.

Scrape eggplant pulp from skin into colander and let drain. Transfer eggplant to processor. Add oil, lemon juice, 2 tablespoons oregano and cumin. Puree until smooth. Season with salt and pepper. Cool completely. (*Can be prepared 1 day ahead. Cover and refrigerate.*)

Line platter with lettuce. Halve tomato slices and arrange around edge of platter. Cut pita into wedges and arrange around platter. Mound eggplant mixture in center. Sprinkle with oregano.

Tofu and Mushrooms with Indonesian-Style Sauce

Begin marinating this delicious and unusual appetizer one day before serving.

4 servings

Sauce
½ cup tamari soy sauce*
¼ cup firmly packed light brown
sugar
3 tablespoons light corn syrup
2 teaspoons light unsulfured
molasses
½ teaspoon minced fresh ginger

Tofu
1 pound firm tofu

2 large dried shiitake
mushrooms (about ¼ ounce),
stemmed, caps broken into
small pieces

½ cup water
¼ cup olive oil
¼ cup Sherry wine vinegar or red
wine vinegar
¼ cup dry red wine
¼ cup tamari soy sauce
1 garlic clove, halved
1 teaspoon dried oregano,
crumbled
¼ teaspoon salt
⅛ teaspoon pepper

Toasted sesame seeds
Cilantro sprigs

For sauce: Whisk all ingredients in small bowl to blend. (*Can be prepared 3 days ahead. Cover and refrigerate.*)

For tofu: Cut tofu into 1-inch-thick slices. Drain between several layers of paper towels for 30 minutes. Place slices in single layer in shallow pan.

Bring mushrooms and water to boil in heavy small saucepan. Continue boiling until mushrooms are very tender and liquid is reduced to 2 tablespoons, about 5 minutes. Add remaining ingredients except sesame seeds and cilantro and bring to boil. Reduce heat and simmer 3 minutes. Pour marinade over tofu. Cover and refrigerate overnight.

Prepare barbecue (medium-high heat) or preheat broiler. Remove tofu from marinade and pat dry. Grill or broil until just heated through, turning once, about 5 minutes. Transfer to platter. Drizzle tofu with sauce. Sprinkle with toasted sesame seeds, garnish with fresh cilantro and serve.

*Available at specialty foods stores and natural foods stores.

2 ❦ Soups and Salads

If you're lucky enough to own a perfect little black dress (or, say, a tie that complements every suit in your closet), then you know what versatility means: It works anywhere, everywhere, almost anytime. This trait is shared by soups and salads, as versatile in menus as the little black dress is in wardrobes. Consider the salad, which makes a light appetizer, a refreshing side dish or a tasty entrée. Soups, too, also work as first-course and main-dish fare.

Here, you'll find first-course soups, such as Squash Soup with Prosciutto and Figs, and Garlic and Saffron Soup, along with hearty main-course versions of the same, among them Chicken Soup with Wild Mushrooms and Herbed Matzo Balls as well as Smoked Turkey, Broccoli and Black Bean Soup. Serve the former when you want a light, nonfilling beginning to a sophisticated meal; the latter when you have in mind a satisfying, simple supper that needs only bread and a salad.

And you'll find a number of fine side-dish salad candidates in this chapter, too, including Mixed Green Salad with Lemon Vinaigrette, and Frisée and Radish Salad with Goat Cheese Croutons. In addition, look for some new variations on old favorites, like the colorful New York Potato Salad (mixed with green and red bell peppers, celery and hard-boiled eggs) and Caesar Salad with Onion Bagel Croutons.

Salad for supper is one quick way to solve the problem of a fast, fresh dinner after work or at the end of any busy day. Try Curried Smoked Turkey and Fruit Salad, which is a snap to prepare, or Southern-Style Chicken Salad, enlived with buttermilk, grapes and toasted pecans.

 Soups

Squash Soup with Prosciutto and Figs

8 servings

Soup

- 2 small butternut squash (about 3 pounds total)
- ½ cup water
- ¼ cup (½ stick) butter
- 3 onions, thinly sliced
- 1 teaspoon ground ginger
- 4 cups chicken stock or canned broth
- 1 cup whipping cream
- ½ teaspoon cayenne pepper

Fig Cream

- 9 dried figs
- ¾ cup chilled whipping cream
- 4½ teaspoons dark rum

- Ground nutmeg
- 4 thin prosciutto slices, cut into matchstick-size strips
- Chopped fresh chives

For soup: Preheat oven to 375°F. Cut squash in half. Pour water into baking pan. Place squash cut side down in pan. Bake until tender, about 45 minutes.

Meanwhile, melt butter in heavy large saucepan over medium-low heat. Add sliced onions and ground ginger. Sauté until onions are very tender, about 12 minutes. Transfer onion mixture to processor.

Scoop cooked squash from skin and place in processor. Add 2 cups chicken stock and puree until smooth. Return puree to saucepan. Add remaining 2 cups stock, whipping cream and cayenne pepper. *(Can be prepared 1 day ahead. Cover soup and refrigerate.)*

For fig cream: Bring small saucepan of water to boil. Add figs and simmer until tender, about 30 minutes. Drain. Transfer figs to blender or food processor. Puree until smooth. Beat cream and rum in medium bowl until soft peaks form. Fold in fig puree. Set aside.

Bring soup to simmer over medium heat. Season to taste with nutmeg, salt and pepper. Ladle into bowls. Using 2 spoons, form fig mixture into mounds and float mounds atop soup. Garnish squash soup with prosciutto strips and chopped fresh chives and serve.

Gingered Fish and Watercress Soup

4 servings

- ½ ounce dried Chinese black mushrooms or dried shiitake mushrooms
- ½ cup hot water
- 1½ teaspoons peanut oil
- 1 teaspoon oriental sesame oil
- 3 green onions, minced
- 2 large garlic cloves, minced
- 1 tablespoon plus 1 teaspoon minced peeled fresh ginger
- 3 cups canned low-salt chicken broth
- ¼ cup bottled clam juice
- 1 tablespoon dry Sherry
- 1 tablespoon soy sauce
- ½ pound catfish or other white-fleshed fish fillets, cut into ¾-inch cubes
- 3 large bunches watercress, trimmed

Soak mushrooms in ½ cup hot water until softened, about 20 minutes. Drain mushrooms, reserving soaking liquid. Squeeze out excess moisture. Thinly slice mushroom caps, discarding stems.

Heat peanut oil and sesame oil in heavy large saucepan over medium heat. Add green onions, garlic and ginger and sauté until just tender, about 3 minutes. Add sliced mushrooms and sauté until mushrooms are tender, about 3 minutes. Add chicken broth, mushroom soaking liquid, clam juice, Sherry and soy sauce. Bring to boil. Stir in catfish and watercress and boil until fish is just cooked through, about 2 minutes. Serve immediately.

Chicken Soup with Wild Mushrooms and Herbed Matzo Balls

8 servings

Soup
- 1 tablespoon vegetable oil
- 1 3-pound chicken, cut into pieces
- 2 large onions, cut into 1-inch pieces
- 12 cups water
- 3 celery stalks, cut into 1-inch pieces
- 3 fresh parsley sprigs
- 2 bay leaves

Matzo Balls
- 1 ounce dried shiitake mushrooms
- 2 cups hot water

- ⅓ cup chicken fat (reserved from stock or purchased)

- 4 large eggs
- 2 tablespoons chopped fresh chives
- 1½ tablespoons minced fresh tarragon or 1½ teaspoons dried, crumbled
- 1½ teaspoons salt
- ¼ teaspoon pepper
- 1 cup unsalted matzo meal

- 3½ quarts water (14 cups)

- 1 teaspoon minced fresh tarragon or ¼ teaspoon dried, crumbled
- Minced fresh chives

For soup: Heat oil in heavy large pot over medium-high heat. Add chicken and onions and cook until brown, stirring frequently, about 15 minutes. Add 12 cups water, celery, parsley and bay leaves. Bring to boil, skimming surface. Bring to boil, skimming surface. Reduce heat and simmer gently until reduced to 8 cups, about 5 hours. Strain into bowl. Cover and refrigerate until fat solidifies on top. *(Can be prepared 2 days ahead.)*

Remove fat from soup and reserve fat for matzo balls.

For matzo balls: Place shiitake mushrooms in small bowl. Pour 2 cups hot water over. Let soak until softened, about 30 minutes.

Melt ⅓ cup chicken fat and cool. Combine melted chicken fat, ¼ cup shiitake soaking liquid (reserve remainder), eggs, 2 tablespoons chives, 1½ tablespoons tarragon, 1½ teaspoons salt and ¼ teaspoon pepper in medium bowl and beat to blend. Mix in matzo meal. Cover and refrigerate 3 hours. *(Can be prepared 1 day ahead. Cover mushrooms in soaking liquid and refrigerate.)*

Measure 3½ quarts water into large pot. Salt generously and bring to boil. With dampened hands, form cold matzo meal mixture into 1-inch balls and add to boiling water. Cover and boil until matzo balls are cooked through and tender, about 40 minutes. (To test for doneness, remove 1 matzo ball and cut open.) Transfer matzo balls to plate, using slotted spoon. *(Can be prepared 1 day ahead. Cover tightly and refrigerate.)*

Drain mushrooms, reserving liquid. Thinly slice mushrooms, discarding stems. Combine remaining mushroom soaking liquid, mushrooms, chicken soup and 1 teaspoon fresh tarragon in heavy large saucepan and bring to simmer. Season to taste with salt and pepper. Add matzo balls and simmer until heated through. Ladle soup into bowls. Garnish with chives and serve.

Cream of Spinach Soup

This soup can also be served chilled.

2 to 4 servings

1 10-ounce package frozen spinach soufflé, thawed
1 10½-ounce can cream of potato soup
1½ cups milk

¼ cup sour cream
1 green onion, sliced
1 teaspoon fresh lemon juice
Pinch of dried thyme
Pepper

Place all ingredients in blender and blend until smooth. Transfer to heavy large saucepan. Bring soup to boil over medium-high heat, stirring frequently. Ladle soup into bowls and serve immediately.

Smoked Chicken and Three-Pepper Consommé

The egg whites are used to clarify the stock. When it is gently heated, they rise to the surface, bringing all other particles with them to form a "raft." Care must be taken not to disturb the raft when straining the consommé.

8 servings

12 cups chicken stock or canned broth
8 ounces ground chicken
4 ounces smoked chicken or smoked turkey, finely chopped
1 cup chopped celery
1 cup chopped leeks
⅔ cup chopped carrot
⅔ cup chopped tomato
10 white peppercorns
2 bay leaves
1 bunch fresh thyme (about ½ ounce) or 2 teaspoons dried, crumbled

½ bunch fresh cilantro
1½ teaspoons minced fresh basil or 1 teaspoon dried, crumbled
5 large egg whites

½ red bell pepper
½ green bell pepper
½ yellow bell pepper
2 ounces smoked chicken or turkey
⅓ cup chopped fresh cilantro
4 serrano chilies,* seeded, minced
1 tablespoon sliced pickled ginger**

Place first 12 ingredients in large pot. Beat egg whites in small bowl until just frothy. Add whites to pot and whisk to combine thoroughly. Bring mixture to simmer over medium-low heat; *do not boil.* Turn heat to low and cook until egg white mixture solidifies on surface and broth is clear, approximately 1 hour 45 minutes; *do not stir broth.*

Set strainer lined with several layers of dampened cheesecloth atop large bowl. Using ladle, gently part egg white mixture. Carefully ladle consommé into strainer; do not press on solids in cheesecloth. If any particles clog cheesecloth, remove them and continue ladling. (*Can be prepared 2 days ahead. Cover consommé with plastic and refrigerate.*)

Cut bell peppers and smoked chicken into matchstick-size strips. Reheat consommé in saucepan. Ladle into bowls. Garnish with bell peppers, smoked chicken, cilantro, chilies and ginger.

*A very hot, small fresh green chili available at Latin American markets and some supermarkets.
**Available at oriental markets and in the refrigerated section of some supermarkets.

Onion Soup Gratinée

4 servings

3 tablespoons unsalted butter
1½ pounds yellow onions, thinly sliced
6 tablespoons dry red wine
3 tablespoons dry Sherry
5 cups beef stock or canned broth
1 teaspoon Worcestershire sauce
1 teaspoon dried thyme, crumbled
½ teaspoon dried oregano, crumbled
½ teaspoon white pepper
1 bay leaf

2 shallots or green onions, thinly sliced
2 green onions, thinly sliced
1 large garlic clove, minced

8 toasted French bread baguette slices
8 slices Gruyère cheese

Melt 2 tablespoons butter in heavy large pot over medium-high heat. Add yellow onions and cook until very soft and caramelized, stirring frequently, about 40 minutes. Add wine and Sherry and bring to boil, scraping up any browned bits. Add stock, Worcestershire, thyme, oregano, pepper and bay leaf. Reduce heat and simmer soup 30 minutes, stirring occasionally.

Melt remaining 1 tablespoon butter in heavy medium skillet over medium heat. Add shallots, green onions and garlic and cook until golden, stirring frequently, about 10 minutes. Add to soup and stir to combine. (*Can be prepared 1 day ahead. Cover and refrigerate. Bring to simmer before continuing.*)

Preheat broiler. Ladle soup into 4 broilerproof soup crocks. Top each with 2 toasted bread slices and 2 cheese slices. Broil until cheese bubbles.

Smoked Turkey, Broccoli and Black Bean Soup

A hearty main-course soup for chilly nights.

6 servings

¼ cup (½ stick) unsalted butter
1 cup peeled diced broccoli stems
½ cup chopped carrot
½ cup chopped onion
½ cup chopped celery
2 teaspoons dried thyme, crumbled
2 teaspoons dried oregano, crumbled
1 teaspoon dried basil, crumbled
¼ cup dry white wine
4 cups chicken stock or canned broth

2 cups broccoli florets
1 16-ounce can black beans, drained
8 ounces smoked turkey or smoked chicken, diced
1 tablespoon Worcestershire sauce
½ teaspoon hot pepper sauce (such as Tabasco)
2 cups whipping cream
2 tablespoons cornstarch
2 tablespoons water

Melt butter in heavy large saucepan over medium-high heat. Add broccoli stems, carrot, onion and celery and sauté 5 minutes. Add thyme, oregano and basil and sauté 5 minutes. Add wine and bring to boil. Add stock and cook until liquid is reduced by half, stirring occasionally, about 15 minutes.

Add broccoli florets, beans, turkey, Worcestershire and hot pepper sauces to soup and simmer 5 minutes, stirring occasionally. Add cream and simmer 5 minutes. Season to taste with salt and pepper. (*Can be prepared 2 days ahead. Cover and refrigerate. Rewarm over medium heat before continuing.*) Mix cornstarch with water in small bowl until smooth. Add to soup and cook until soup thickens, stirring occasionally, about 3 minutes.

Sausage and Corn Chowder

6 servings

3 ears fresh corn
4 cups whipping cream
2 cups chicken stock or canned broth
4 garlic cloves, minced
10 fresh thyme sprigs
1 bay leaf
1½ onions, finely chopped

½ pound hot Italian sausage

2 tablespoons (¼ stick) unsalted butter
2 teaspoons minced jalapeño chilies with seeds
½ teaspoon ground cumin
2 tablespoons all purpose flour
2 medium russet potatoes, peeled, cut into 1-inch cubes
1½ teaspoons chopped fresh chives

Cut corn from cob using small sharp knife. Place cobs in large saucepan; set kernels aside. Add cream, stock, garlic, thyme, bay leaf and ⅓ of onions to pan. Simmer 1 hour, stirring occasionally. Strain through sieve set over large bowl, pressing on solids with back of spoon. Set corn stock aside.

Cook sausage in heavy large skillet over medium heat until cooked through, turning occasionally. Cool sausage; cut into 1-inch pieces.

Melt butter in heavy large saucepan over medium heat. Add remaining ⅔ of onions, chilies and cumin and sauté 5 minutes. Add flour and stir 2 minutes. Gradually whisk in corn stock. Add sausage and potatoes. Cover and cook until potatoes are tender, about 25 minutes. Add corn and cook until just tender, stirring occasionally, about 5 minutes. Season to taste with salt and pepper. (*Can be prepared 1 day ahead. Cover and refrigerate. Rewarm over low heat before continuing, thinning with additional chicken stock if necessary.*) Ladle chowder into bowls. Sprinkle with chopped chives and serve.

Garlic and Saffron Soup

4 servings

5 tablespoons olive oil
2 cups trimmed sourdough bread cubes
4 large garlic cloves, quartered
⅓ cup dry white wine
4 cups canned low-salt chicken broth
2 generous pinches saffron threads

8 ½-inch-thick French bread baguette slices
½ cup grated Manchego* or Monterey Jack cheese
Minced fresh chives or green onion tops
Saffron threads

Heat 4 tablespoons oil in heavy large skillet over medium-high heat. Add bread cubes and garlic and sauté until bread is light golden, about 4 minutes. Add wine, then broth and saffron; bring to boil. Reduce heat, cover and simmer 25 minutes. Puree soup in blender. Return soup to saucepan. Season with salt.

Preheat oven to 350°F. Arrange French bread slices on cookie sheet. Brush with remaining 1 tablespoon oil. Bake until lightly toasted, about 8 minutes. Sprinkle cheese over croutons. Transfer cookie sheet to broiler; broil croutons until cheese melts. Place 2 croutons in each bowl. Bring soup to simmer. Ladle over croutons. Sprinkle with chives and a few saffron threads and serve.

*A Spanish sheep's-milk cheese available at cheese shops, Spanish markets and specialty foods stores.

Shrimp Gazpacho

6 servings

2 garlic cloves, chopped
2 tablespoons olive oil
2 tablespoons red wine vinegar
2 tablespoons fresh lemon juice
½ pound cooked large shrimp, peeled, deveined

¾ pound large plum tomatoes (about 6), seeded, chopped
1 green bell pepper, chopped

1 red bell pepper, chopped
½ large cucumber, peeled, seeded, chopped
1 bunch green onions, chopped
½ bunch fresh cilantro leaves, chopped
1 large jalapeño chili, minced
4½ cups tomato juice, chilled
Lemon wedges

Combine first 4 ingredients in medium bowl. Add shrimp; cover mixture and refrigerate 1 to 2 hours.

Combine tomatoes, green and red bell peppers, cucumber, green onions, cilantro and jalapeño in large bowl. Add tomato juice. Stir in shrimp mixture. Season to taste with salt and pepper. *(Can be prepared 6 hours ahead. Cover and refrigerate.)* Ladle soup into bowls. Garnish with lemon wedges and serve.

❦ *Side-Dish Salads*

Greek Salad

8 servings

½ head romaine lettuce, torn into pieces
½ head iceberg lettuce, torn into pieces
1 cucumber, peeled, sliced
1 bell pepper, sliced
½ red onion, thinly sliced
2 celery stalks, chopped
1 large tomato, diced

½ cup sliced black olives
8 ounces feta cheese, crumbled
⅔ cup purchased olive oil and vinegar dressing
½ teaspoon dried oregano, crumbled
½ teaspoon dried dillweed
½ teaspoon pepper

Combine first 8 ingredients in large salad bowl. Sprinkle with feta. Whisk salad dressing, herbs and pepper in small bowl to blend. Pour over salad. Toss well.

Romaine Salad with Anchovy Vinaigrette

2 servings

1 tablespoon fresh lemon juice
1 teaspoon Dijon mustard
¼ cup olive oil
4 anchovies, chopped

⅓ large head romaine lettuce, torn into bite-size pieces

Combine lemon juice and mustard in small bowl. Gradually whisk in olive oil. Add chopped anchovies. Season dressing with salt and pepper.

Place lettuce in large bowl. Add dressing and toss to coat.

Mixed Green Salad with Lemon Vinaigrette

10 servings

2 shallots, finely chopped
2 tablespoons fresh lemon juice
1 tablespoon Dijon mustard
1 tablespoon white wine vinegar
1 teaspoon grated lemon peel
¾ cup olive oil

2 heads Boston or butter lettuce, torn into bite-size pieces

1 head radicchio, torn into bite-size pieces
1 bunch watercress, tough stems trimmed
1 bunch arugula
1 cucumber, peeled, thinly sliced
2 celery stalks, thinly sliced
⅔ cup grated Parmesan cheese

Whisk first 5 ingredients in small bowl. Gradually whisk in oil. Season with salt and pepper. (*Can be prepared 1 day ahead. Refrigerate. Re-whisk before using.*)

Combine all remaining ingredients except cheese in large bowl. Add enough dressing to season to taste and toss well. Sprinkle with cheese and toss gently. Divide among plates and serve.

Caesar Salad with Onion Bagel Croutons

Bagel croutons are a nice twist for a classic salad.

8 servings

½ cup olive oil
2 tablespoons red wine vinegar
2 tablespoons fresh lemon juice
1 tablespoon Worcestershire sauce
1 teaspoon Dijon mustard
1 teaspoon grated lemon peel
1 large garlic clove, minced

2 drops hot pepper sauce (such as Tabasco)
2 heads romaine lettuce, torn into bite-size pieces
Onion Bagel Croutons (see recipe)
⅔ cup grated Parmesan cheese (about 3 ounces)

Whisk first 8 ingredients in small bowl. Combine lettuce, as many croutons as desired, cheese and generous amount of pepper in large bowl. Add dressing, toss thoroughly and serve immediately.

Onion Bagel Croutons

Makes about 4 cups

3 tablespoons butter
1½ tablespoons olive oil
2 small garlic cloves, minced

3 onion bagels, each cut into 2 semicircles

Preheat oven to 325°F. Combine first 3 ingredients in heavy small saucepan over medium heat. Stir until butter melts. Remove from heat. Slice bagel into ¼-inch-thick rounds. Place on cookie sheet. Brush with butter mixture. Bake until crisp and brown, about 30 minutes. Cool. (*Can be prepared 1 week ahead. Store in airtight container at room temperature.*)

Green Bean and Roasted Garlic Salad

A crisp and tangy side-dish salad. The garlic cloves are roasted to mellow their assertive flavor.

8 servings

2 red bell peppers

1 pound green beans (preferably haricots verts), halved

8 tablespoons olive oil

4 elephant garlic cloves or large garlic cloves, peeled

2½ tablespoons balsamic vinegar or 1 tablespoon red wine vinegar

2 tablespoons fresh lime juice

6 cups torn mixed greens such as radicchio, Belgian endive, Bibb lettuce or arugula

2 tablespoons chopped fresh basil

2 tablespoons toasted pine nuts

Char bell peppers over gas flame or in broiler until blackened on all sides. Place in paper bag and let stand 10 minutes to steam. Peel, seed and thinly slice bell peppers. Set aside.

Cook green beans in large pot of boiling water until just tender but still firm to bite. Drain. Refresh under cold water. Drain beans well.

Preheat oven to 350°F. Heat 2 tablespoons olive oil in heavy small ovenproof skillet over medium heat. Add whole garlic cloves and sauté until golden brown on all sides, turning occasionally, about 8 minutes. Cover skillet with lid. Transfer skillet to oven and cook until garlic cloves are tender, about 10 minutes. Cool. Chop garlic. (*Can be prepared 1 day ahead. Cover and refrigerate bell peppers, beans and garlic separately.*)

Whisk remaining 6 tablespoons olive oil, vinegar and 2 tablespoons fresh lime juice in small bowl. Place mixed greens in large bowl. Toss with just enough dressing to season to taste. Divide mixed greens among plates. Add roasted bell peppers, green beans, garlic, chopped fresh basil and toasted pine nuts to remaining dressing and toss to combine. Season to taste with salt and pepper. Place green bean mixture atop mixed greens on plates and serve.

Dreaming-of-Spring Salad

A composed salad that features all the bright and pretty colors of the season.

6 servings

⅓ cup walnut oil or other nut oil

2 medium shallots, minced

2 tablespoons fresh pink grapefruit juice

¼ teaspoon sugar

3 pink grapefruits

3 heads Belgian endive

1 head radicchio, thinly sliced

2 avocados, peeled, pitted

¼ cup chopped fresh chives

Toasted chopped walnuts

Whisk first 4 ingredients together in small bowl. Season dressing to taste with salt and white pepper. Set aside.

Using small sharp knife, remove peel and white pith from grapefruits. Working over large bowl to catch juices, cut between membranes to release segments. Squeeze juice from membranes into bowl. Reserve juice and segments separately. Trim base from endive heads and separate into spears. (*Can be prepared 1 day ahead. Cover dressing, grapefruit juice and endive separately; chill.*)

Place sliced radicchio on platter. Arrange endive spears in rows atop radicchio. Thinly slice avocados. Dip avocado slices into reserved grapefruit juice. Fill each endive spear with 1 avocado slice and top with 1 grapefruit segment. Whisk chopped fresh chives into dressing and drizzle over salad. Sprinkle with walnuts.

Lentil, Mint and Feta Cheese Salad

6 servings

1½ cups lentils, rinsed, drained
1 bay leaf
½ cup diced carrot
¼ cup chopped red onion
¾ cup Lemon Vinaigrette (see recipe)
½ yellow or red bell pepper, diced

1 tablespoon minced fresh mint
1 tablespoon minced fresh parsley
1 garlic clove, minced
4 ounces crumbled feta cheese
   (about 1 cup)

Place lentils and bay leaf in large pot. Add enough water to cover lentils by 4 inches. Bring to boil, reduce heat and simmer until lentils are tender yet still retain shape, about 20 minutes. Add carrot and red onion and continue cooking 1 minute. Remove from heat and drain. Transfer lentil mixture to large bowl. Stir in vinaigrette, bell pepper, mint, parsley and garlic. Cool slightly. Add feta and toss well. Season with salt and pepper. (*Can be prepared 1 day ahead. Cover and refrigerate.*) Serve chilled or at room temperature.

Lemon Vinaigrette

Makes about ¾ cup

½ cup olive oil
2 tablespoons fresh lemon juice
1 tablespoon Champagne vinegar or
   white wine vinegar

2 teaspoons grated lemon peel
½ teaspoon salt
¼ teaspoon pepper

Whisk all ingredients to blend in small bowl. (*Vinaigrette can be prepared up to 2 days ahead. Cover and refrigerate.*)

Frisée and Radish Salad with Goat Cheese Croutons

Frisée is the French word for curly endive.

4 servings

2 tablespoons Sherry vinegar
2 teaspoons Dijon mustard
1 shallot or green onion, minced
⅓ cup olive oil
1 small head curly endive, torn into
   bite-size pieces
1 bunch radishes, trimmed, thinly
   sliced

12 ½-inch-thick slices French bread
   baguette
   Olive oil
4 ounces soft fresh goat cheese
   (such as Montrachet)

Combine vinegar, mustard and shallot in small bowl. Whisk in ⅓ cup oil. Season dressing to taste with salt and pepper. Combine endive and radishes in large bowl. (*Can be prepared 4 hours ahead. Cover salad with damp towel and refrigerate. Cover dressing and let stand at room temperature.*)

Preheat broiler. Broil 1 side of bread until golden brown. Brush second side with olive oil. Season with salt and pepper. Spread with goat cheese. Season with pepper. Broil until bread is brown. Cut each slice into quarters.

Add dressing to salad and toss to coat. Divide among plates. Top with croutons and serve immediately.

New York Potato Salad

8 servings

3 pounds russet potatoes

2 tablespoons white wine vinegar
1½ teaspoons dry mustard
¾ cup mayonnaise
½ cup sour cream
2 tablespoons sugar
1½ teaspoons Hungarian hot paprika

1 green bell pepper, diced
1 red bell pepper, diced
2 celery stalks, diced
4 hard-boiled eggs, chilled, shelled and sliced (optional)
Chopped fresh parsley

Cover potatoes with salted water in large pot. Cover and boil gently until potatoes are tender but still hold their shape, about 30 minutes. Drain and cool slightly. Peel and cut into 1-inch pieces. Transfer potato pieces to large bowl.

Stir vinegar and mustard in medium bowl until mustard dissolves. Mix in mayonnaise, sour cream, sugar and paprika. Add bell peppers and celery. Pour dressing over warm potatoes; toss gently. Season with salt and pepper. Cool completely. (*Can be prepared 1 day ahead. Cover and refrigerate.*) Garnish with sliced eggs and chopped parsley. Serve at room temperature.

Main-Dish Salads

Southern-Style Chicken Salad

Buttermilk lends its distinctive tang, grapes impart sweetness and toasted pecans add a delightful richness to this salad. Leftover cooked chicken also works well here; you'll need about 2½ cups. Corn muffins and lemony iced tea with the salad and peach pie for dessert add more southern accents to the meal.

4 servings

Dressing
½ cup mayonnaise
¼ cup minced green onions
3 tablespoons buttermilk
2 tablespoons minced fresh dill or 1 teaspoon dried dillweed
¼ teaspoon pepper

Salad
1 pound boneless skinless chicken breasts (about 4)

1 cup white wine
1 large fresh dill sprig or pinch of dried dillweed
⅛ teaspoon pepper

1½ cups seedless grapes (preferably green and red)
1 cup thinly sliced celery

Bibb lettuce leaves
½ cup pecan pieces, toasted
Fresh dill sprigs (optional)

For dressing: Whisk mayonnaise, green onions, buttermilk, dill and pepper in small bowl to blend. (*Can be made 1 day ahead. Cover and chill.*)

For salad: Arrange chicken in heavy medium skillet. Add wine, dill and pepper. Season with salt. Add water if necessary to cover chicken. Simmer until chicken is just cooked through, turning once, about 11 minutes. Transfer chicken to plate and cool completely.

Cut chicken into ½-inch pieces. Place in large bowl. Add grapes and celery. Mix in enough dressing to coat mixture thoroughly. Reserve remaining dressing. Season salad to taste with salt and pepper. Refrigerate at least 20 minutes to develop flavors. (*Can be prepared 3 hours ahead. Cover and refrigerate.*)

Arrange lettuce leaves on plates. Mound salad in leaves. Sprinkle pecans over. Garnish each salad with fresh dill sprigs. Pass reserved dressing separately.

Curried Smoked Turkey and Fruit Salad

This refreshing dish is perfect for a luncheon and is a snap to prepare. You can purchase thick slices of smoked turkey at your local delicatessen.

6 to 8 servings

1 pound smoked or cooked turkey, cut into ¾-inch cubes
¾ pound green seedless grapes, stemmed
1 large cantaloupe, peeled, cubed
3 cups sliced celery (about 4 stalks)
6 green onions, sliced

½ cup golden raisins
½ cup mayonnaise
⅓ cup plain yogurt
⅓ cup sour cream
1 tablespoon curry powder

Curly lettuce leaves
1 cup sliced almonds, toasted

Combine turkey, grapes, cantaloupe, celery, green onions and raisins in large bowl. Whisk mayonnaise, yogurt, sour cream and curry powder together in small bowl. Pour mayonnaise mixture over salad and toss thoroughly. Season salad to taste with salt and pepper.

Line platter with lettuce leaves. Spoon salad atop lettuce. Sprinkle sliced almonds over salad and serve immediately.

Lobster and Artichoke Heart Salad with Lemon Dressing

2 servings

Salad
1 cup dry white wine
1 carrot, peeled, cut into small pieces
½ onion, quartered
5 fresh thyme sprigs or 1 teaspoon dried, crumbled
1 teaspoon fennel seeds
1 1½-pound live lobster

1 lemon, halved
4 artichokes

3 cups water
1 tablespoon white wine vinegar
1 teaspoon all purpose flour

Dressing
1 cup mayonnaise
3½ tablespoons fresh lemon juice
3 tablespoons chopped fresh chives
1 tablespoon chopped fresh tarragon or 1 teaspoon dried, crumbled
½ cup whipping cream

8 cups mixed greens, torn into pieces
Fresh tarragon sprigs (optional)

For salad: Combine first 5 ingredients in large pot. Add enough water to almost fill pot. Bring to boil. Add lobster and cook until shell is red and lobster meat is just cooked, about 10 minutes. Transfer lobster to platter and cool. Remove tail and claw meat from lobster. (*Can be prepared 1 day ahead. Refrigerate.*)

Fill medium bowl with water. Squeeze in juice of ½ lemon. Cut stem off 1 artichoke and rub exposed area with remaining lemon half. Starting from base, bend each leaf off at natural break. Cut off tight cone of leaves above heart. Scoop out and discard choke. Trim off all dark areas of heart with small knife. Add artichoke heart to acidulated water. Repeat with remaining artichokes.

Bring 3 cups water, 1 tablespoon white wine vinegar and flour to boil in heavy medium saucepan. Add artichoke hearts and simmer until hearts are tender, about 20 minutes. Let cool in cooking liquid. (*Can be prepared 3 hours ahead. Let stand at room temperature.*)

For dressing: Mix mayonnaise, lemon juice, chives and tarragon in medium bowl. Season to taste with salt and pepper. Whip cream in another bowl until medium-firm peaks form. Fold cream into mayonnaise mixture. Cover and refrigerate. (*Can be prepared up to 3 hours ahead.*)

Slice lobster thinly. Remove artichoke hearts from liquid and pat dry. Slice thinly. Toss greens with enough dressing to coat. Transfer greens to platter. Arrange sliced lobster and artichoke hearts atop greens. Moisten with some dressing. Garnish with tarragon sprigs. Serve, passing remaining dressing.

Couscous and Chick-Pea Salad

Tossed with a refreshing mint vinaigrette, this salad includes feta cheese, chickpeas, black olives and flavorful vegetables. It's fun to eat in the traditional manner: Just roll up a scoop of salad in a lettuce leaf. Start off with an "aperitif" of tomato juice or vegetable juice, then accompany the salad with pita triangles. A fitting finale to the meal? Purchased baklava.

4 servings

Salad
1¾ cups water
½ teaspoon salt
1 cup couscous (about 6 ounces)
1 15-ounce can chick-peas (garbanzo beans), drained
2 small red bell peppers, diced
4 green onions, thinly sliced
½ cup finely chopped carrots
½ cup diced pitted brine-cured olives, such as Kalamata (about 4 ounces)

Mint Vinaigrette
¾ cup leafy fresh mint-sprig tops (about 1½ bunches)
3 tablespoons white wine vinegar
1 garlic clove
1 teaspoon Dijon mustard
¼ teaspoon sugar
⅔ cup olive oil

6 ounces feta cheese, coarsely crumbled

Romaine lettuce leaves
Fresh mint sprigs (optional)

For salad: Bring water and salt to boil in medium saucepan. Add couscous. Remove saucepan from heat; cover and let stand 5 minutes. Transfer couscous to large bowl. Fluff with fork. Add chick-peas, red peppers, green onions, carrots and olives to bowl.

For vinaigrette: Finely chop ¾ cup mint with vinegar, garlic, mustard and sugar in processor, using on/off turns. With machine running, gradually add olive oil. Process until well blended.

Pour dressing over salad. Toss to distribute vegetables and dressing evenly. Gently mix in feta cheese. Season with salt and pepper. (*Can be prepared 6 hours ahead. Cover and refrigerate.*)

Arrange lettuce leaves around edge of large platter. Mound salad in center. Garnish salad with fresh mint sprigs.

Warm Lamb Salad with Mixed Greens

An elegant dish. You can reheat leftover lamb to use here instead of the sautéed.

6 servings

½ cup olive oil
½ cup vegetable oil
½ cup chopped fresh mint
½ cup chopped fresh basil
¼ cup balsamic vinegar or 3 tablespoons red wine vinegar
2 large shallots, halved
2 large garlic cloves, halved
1 teaspoon Dijon mustard
1 teaspoon salt
¼ teaspoon sugar

12 ounces lamb leg meat, trimmed, cut into 1¼ × ⅓-inch strips
7 cups torn mixed greens, such as radicchio and red leaf lettuce
1 9-ounce package frozen artichoke hearts, thawed, patted dry
1 large red bell pepper, cut into matchstick-size strips
10 ounces mushrooms, sliced
½ cup fresh mint leaves
½ cup fresh basil leaves
Fresh basil sprigs
Fresh mint sprigs

Blend first 10 ingredients in blender or processor until dressing is as smooth as possible. (*Can be prepared 1 day ahead. Cover and refrigerate.*)

Heat ¼ cup dressing in heavy large skillet over medium-high heat. Add lamb and cook, stirring frequently, about 3 minutes for medium-rare. Drain. Transfer to bowl. Season with salt and pepper. Combine greens, artichokes, bell pepper, mushrooms, ½ cup mint and ½ cup basil in bowl. Add enough dressing to season to taste and toss gently. Mound salads on plates. Top with lamb. Garnish with basil and mint sprigs.

Tropical Chicken Salad

4 servings

4 boneless chicken breasts

¼ cup olive oil
3 tablespoons red wine vinegar
1 teaspoon Dijon mustard
¼ teaspoon dried rubbed sage
6 cups salad greens

1 papaya, peeled, seeded, chopped
1 mango, peeled, pitted, chopped
1 6-ounce basket raspberries
1 tablespoon minced fresh mint
½ cup chopped toasted walnuts

Preheat oven to 425°F. Place chicken in baking pan. Season generously with salt and pepper. Bake until cooked through, about 20 minutes. Cool completely; cut chicken into bite-size pieces.

Whisk olive oil, vinegar, mustard and sage to blend in small bowl. Combine chicken, salad greens, papaya, mango, raspberries and mint in large bowl. Add dressing and toss well. Divide mixture among 4 plates. Sprinkle with walnuts.

Seafood, Avocado and Hearts of Palm Salad

12 servings

Dressing
1½ cups sour cream
1½ cups mayonnaise
½ cup fresh lime juice
5 green onions, chopped
3 jalapeño chilies, seeded, minced
1¼ teaspoons chili powder
¾ teaspoon dry mustard

Salad
3 7½-ounce cans hearts of palm, drained
3 large tomatoes
3 large avocados, peeled, pitted
Red leaf lettuce leaves
2½ pounds cooked medium shrimp, peeled, deveined
24 cooked crab claws

For dressing: Combine sour cream, mayonnaise, fresh lime juice, green onions, jalapeños, chili powder and dry mustard in medium bowl. Season to taste with salt. (*Can be prepared 2 days ahead. Cover and refrigerate.*)

For salad: Cut hearts of palm, tomatoes and avocados into 1-inch pieces. Combine in medium bowl. Mix vegetables with just enough dressing to coat lightly. Line large platter with lettuce leaves. Mound vegetables in center. Surround with shrimp and crab. Serve remaining dressing on side.

3 ❦ *Pasta, Pizza and Sandwiches*

Most of us probably discovered pasta, pizza and sandwiches back when we were kids. Now *that* pasta was probably spaghetti and meatballs, the pizza was plain cheese and the sandwiches were peanut butter and jelly, but they all made good eating. And while our tastes may have grown up somewhat and our culinary horizons widened, pasta, pizza and sandwiches are still favorites all around.

If you miss the spaghetti of your childhood, try Cheese Ravioli with Old-fashioned Meat Sauce, a more sophisticated take on that classic, and quick and easy to make, too. Pasta with Spinach, Sausage and Roquefort Cream Sauce is another possibility, a rich and delicious main course. Some terrific first-course and side-dish pastas round out the selection.

If you're older than six, it's a good bet that you like more than cheese on your pizza these days, so try the Shallot and Garlic Pizza with Two Cheeses, an innovative pie topped with a fresh tomato and parsley salad. Bobolis, those new baked cheese pizza crusts available at supermarkets, turn up in two easy recipes: Garlicky Eggplant, Tomato and Basil Bobolis and Boboli Pizza with Garlic, Peppers and Goat Cheese.

And even if you don't pack a lunch these days, it's likely you'll find a sandwich here that appeals to you, maybe updated Sloppy Joes on toasted kaiser rolls or quick-to-make Grilled Eggplant and Fontina Sandwiches.

 Pasta

Pasta with Bell Peppers and Sausage

8 servings

¼ cup plus 2 tablespoons olive oil
3 yellow bell peppers, cut into strips
3 red bell peppers, cut into strips
3 green bell peppers, cut into strips
2½ pounds Italian turkey sausage, cut into ½-inch rounds

1 large red onion, chopped
1 large yellow onion, chopped
¾ pound mushrooms, sliced

15 garlic cloves, chopped
1 cup dry white wine
1½ cups chicken stock or canned low-salt broth
¾ cup Dijon mustard

1½ pounds spaghetti or linguine

1½ bunches green onions, chopped
1⅓ cups grated Parmesan cheese (about 5 ounces)

Heat ¼ cup olive oil in heavy large skillet over medium-high heat. Add all peppers and cook until tender, tossing occasionally, about 15 minutes. Transfer peppers to large bowl. Cook turkey sausage in same skillet over medium heat until cooked through, stirring occasionally, about 15 minutes. Transfer turkey sausage to large bowl with peppers using slotted spoon; do not clean skillet.

Add remaining 2 tablespoons olive oil to drippings in skillet. Add red and yellow onions, sliced mushrooms and chopped garlic and sauté over medium heat until vegetables are tender, about 15 minutes. Add dry white wine and bring to boil. Whisk chicken stock and Dijon mustard together. Add stock mixture to skillet and cook until sauce thickens, about 8 minutes. Mix in sausage and bell peppers. (*Sauce can be prepared 1 day ahead. Cover and refrigerate. Bring sauce to simmer before using.*)

Cook pasta in large pot of boiling salted water until just tender but still firm to bite, stirring occasionally. Drain well.

Meanwhile, add green onions and grated Parmesan cheese to sauce and cook over medium heat until heated through, stirring occasionally, about 5 minutes.

Transfer pasta to bowl. Pour sauce over, toss and serve.

Linguine with Arugula, Pine Nuts and Parmesan Cheese

6 servings

1 pound linguine

½ cup olive oil
4 ounces arugula, trimmed

1 cup grated Parmesan cheese
½ cup pine nuts, toasted
Additional grated Parmesan cheese

Cook linguine in large pot of boiling salted water until just tender but still firm to bite, stirring occasionally.

Meanwhile, heat oil in heavy large skillet over medium heat. Add arugula and stir until just wilted, about 30 seconds. Remove from heat.

Drain pasta and return to pot. Add arugula and toss well. Add 1 cup Parmesan and salt and pepper to taste; toss well. Transfer to bowl. Sprinkle with pine nuts. Serve immediately, passing additional Parmesan separately.

Cheese Ravioli with Old-fashioned Meat Sauce

This recipe makes plenty of sauce for two meals, so enjoy some with this dish and freeze the remainder for another time. The sauce is also great over tortellini, penne *or* fusilli. *You can find the convenient prepared ravioli in the refrigerator section of most supermarkets.*

2 servings

1 tablespoon olive oil	1 teaspoon dried oregano, crumbled
1 medium onion, chopped	
¾ pound extra-lean ground beef	⅛ teaspoon dried crushed red pepper
2 large garlic cloves, chopped	
1 28-ounce can Italian plum tomatoes	¾ pound purchased cheese ravioli
1 16-ounce can tomato puree	Grated Parmesan or Romano cheese
1 teaspoon dried basil, crumbled	

Heat oil in heavy medium saucepan over medium heat. Add onion and cook until tender, stirring occasionally, about 8 minutes. Add ground beef and garlic and sauté until meat is no longer pink, breaking up with fork, about 5 minutes. Puree tomatoes with juices in processor. Add to saucepan. Add canned tomato puree, herbs and dried crushed red pepper. Simmer 30 minutes, stirring occasionally. Season sauce with salt and pepper.

Cook pasta in large pot of boiling salted water until just tender but still firm to bite. Drain well. Place pasta in large bowl. Add enough sauce to coat; stir. Serve, passing cheese separately.

Orzo Baked with Greek Cheeses

8 servings

1 14½-ounce can chicken broth	1 tablespoon chopped fresh dill
1 pound orzo or risi pasta	⅓ cup grated kasseri* or Romano cheese
½ cup whipping cream	
¼ cup olive oil	
½ pound feta cheese, crumbled	

Pour broth into large pot. Add enough water to broth to almost fill pot. Add salt and bring to boil. Stir in orzo and boil until just tender but still firm to bite, stirring occasionally. Drain well. Return to pot. Mix in cream, oil, feta and dill. Season with salt and pepper. Transfer to 1½-quart baking dish. (*Can be prepared 1 day ahead. Cover and refrigerate. Bring to room temperature before continuing.*)

Preheat oven to 350°F. Sprinkle orzo with cheese. Bake until heated through, about 40 minutes. Serve immediately.

*A firm white cheese from sheep's milk. Available at Greek markets and specialty foods stores.

Noodles with Poppy Seeds and Peas

2 servings

¼ pound fettuccine or egg noodles	1 tablespoon butter
½ 10-ounce package frozen peas	1 teaspoon poppy seeds

Cook fettuccine in large pot of boiling salted water until almost tender. Add peas and cook until peas and fettuccine are just tender, about 2 minutes. Drain well. Return to pot. Add butter and poppy seeds. Season with salt and pepper and toss to coat. Serve immediately.

Spinach- and Cheese-stuffed Pasta Shells

Fennel seeds add a flavorful new twist to this vegetarian main course.

6 servings

2 10-ounce packages frozen chopped spinach, thawed
15 ounces ricotta cheese
1 cup (about 4 ounces) grated Parmesan cheese
2 tablespoons fennel seeds
2 tablespoons chopped fresh basil or 2 teaspoons dried, crumbled

3 garlic cloves, minced
3½ cups purchased marinara or spaghetti sauce
32 jumbo pasta shells, freshly cooked
Additional grated Parmesan cheese

Squeeze spinach dry. Transfer spinach to large bowl. Add ricotta, ½ cup Parmesan, fennel, basil and garlic to bowl. Season mixture with salt and pepper; blend.

Preheat oven to 350°F. Spoon ½ cup marinara sauce evenly over bottom of 9 × 13 × 2-inch baking dish. Fill each pasta shell with spinach mixture. Place shells, filling side up, in dish. Spoon remaining sauce over shells. Sprinkle with remaining ½ cup Parmesan. Cover loosely with foil and bake until heated through, about 30 minutes. Serve, passing additional Parmesan separately.

Fettuccine with Greens, Raisins and Pine Nuts

4 servings

¼ cup golden raisins
1 bunch green chard
6 tablespoons (¾ stick) unsalted butter
4 garlic cloves, minced
1 bunch spinach, trimmed
1½ teaspoons fresh lemon juice

1 pound fettuccine
1 cup grated Parmesan cheese (about 4 ounces)

⅓ cup toasted pine nuts
1 tablespoon minced fresh chives
2 teaspoons minced fresh thyme or ¾ teaspoon dried, crumbled
2 teaspoons minced fresh marjoram or ¾ teaspoon dried, crumbled
Additional grated Parmesan cheese

Place raisins in small bowl. Add enough hot water to cover. Let stand until plump, about 10 minutes. Drain.

Remove stems and ribs from chard. Thinly slice enough stems to measure ½ cup. Discard remaining stems. Slice chard leaves into ½-inch-wide strips. Melt butter in heavy large skillet over medium heat. Continue cooking butter until golden brown, stirring constantly, about 7 minutes. Add minced garlic and sliced chard leaves and cook until chard is tender and wilted, stirring frequently, about 3 minutes. Add spinach and stir until wilted, about 2 minutes. Stir in raisins and fresh lemon juice.

Meanwhile, bring large pot of salted water to boil. Add fettuccine and ½ cup chard stems to boiling water and cook until pasta is just tender but still firm to bite. Drain pasta and chard stems. Transfer to large bowl. Add spinach mixture, 1 cup grated Parmesan cheese, pine nuts and herbs. Toss thoroughly. Season pasta with salt and pepper. Serve, passing additional Parmesan cheese.

Fettuccine with Smoked Turkey in Black Peppercorn Sauce

2 servings

1 teaspoon butter
1 teaspoon minced shallot
1 teaspoon crushed black peppercorns
¼ cup dry white wine
¾ cup whipping cream
⅛ teaspoon ground nutmeg

4 ounces fettuccine

4 ounces smoked turkey breast, cut into matchstick-size strips
1 tablespoon chopped fresh chives
Grated Parmesan cheese

Melt butter in heavy medium skillet over medium heat. Add shallot and peppercorns and sauté 20 seconds. Add wine and boil until almost no liquid remains in skillet, about 4 minutes. Add cream and nutmeg and boil until reduced to sauce consistency, about 5 minutes. Season sauce with salt.

Meanwhile, cook pasta in large pot of boiling salted water until just tender but still firm to bite, stirring occasionally. Drain. Transfer to bowl.

Add sauce and turkey to pasta and toss thoroughly. Sprinkle with chives. Serve, passing Parmesan cheese separately.

Pasta with Spinach, Sausage and Roquefort Cream Sauce

4 to 6 servings

¼ cup olive oil
4 ounces hot Italian sausage, casings removed
8 ounces mushrooms, sliced
2 bunches fresh spinach, stems trimmed
2 garlic cloves, minced

¼ cup coarsely chopped walnuts
2 cups whipping cream
4 ounces Roquefort cheese
2 teaspoons Dijon mustard

1 pound fettuccine

Heat oil in heavy skillet over medium-high heat. Add sausage and cook until no longer pink, crumbling with fork, about 5 minutes. Transfer sausage to bowl using slotted spoon. Add mushrooms to skillet and sauté 2 minutes. Add spinach and sauté until wilted. Add garlic and walnuts and stir 1 minute. Add cream and Roquefort and bring to boil. Reduce heat and simmer until thickened to sauce consistency, stirring occasionally, about 10 minutes. Add sausage and mustard. Season to taste with salt and pepper. Stir sauce until heated through.

Meanwhile, cook pasta in large pot of boiling salted water until just tender but still firm to bite, stirring occasionally. Drain. Place in large bowl.

Pour sauce over pasta. Toss gently.

Fettuccine and Salmon in Scotch Cream Sauce

2 servings

1 cup whipping cream
1 cup milk
6 tablespoons (¾ stick) unsalted butter
2 tablespoons minced shallots or green onions
1½ tablespoons Scotch whisky
2½ tablespoons all purpose flour

½ pound smoked salmon or lox trimmings, cut into ¼-inch pieces
1 tablespoon finely chopped green onions
1½ teaspoons chopped fresh parsley Pinch of white pepper

8 ounces fettuccine

Scald cream and milk in heavy medium saucepan. Melt butter in heavy large skillet over medium heat. Add shallots and sauté 2 minutes. Remove pan from heat. Add whisky and stir to blend. Return skillet to heat. Sprinkle flour over and stir until golden brown, about 2 minutes. Gradually whisk in cream mixture and cook until thickened, whisking constantly, about 5 minutes. Mix in salmon, green onions, parsley and pepper. Set aside.

Cook pasta in large pot of boiling salted water until just tender but still firm to bite, stirring occasionally. Drain well. Transfer to bowl.

Rewarm sauce over medium heat, whisking constantly. Pour sauce over pasta; toss to coat. Serve immediately.

Spinach Linguine with Goat Cheese

2 servings

3 tablespoons olive oil
1 bunch green onions, sliced
4 plum tomatoes, chopped
1 red bell pepper, chopped
6 oil-packed sun-dried tomatoes, drained, chopped
2 garlic cloves, minced
¼ teaspoon dried oregano, crumbled

1 tablespoon chopped fresh parsley
1 tablespoon chopped fresh basil or 1 teaspoon dried, crumbled
8 ounces spinach linguine or spaghetti, freshly cooked
4 ounces soft goat cheese (such as Montrachet), sliced

Heat oil in heavy large skillet over medium heat. Add next 6 ingredients and sauté until onions are tender, about 15 minutes. Stir in parsley and basil. Season with salt and pepper. Add pasta; toss thoroughly. Divide pasta between 2 plates. Top each with half of goat cheese.

 *Pizza*

Garlicky Eggplant, Tomato and Basil Bobolis

Purchased Boboli crusts make these pizzas a real snap to prepare.

8 servings

4 medium Japanese eggplants, thinly sliced lengthwise
¼ cup olive oil

3 cups grated mozzarella cheese
2 1-pound Bobolis (baked cheese pizza crusts)
1½ pounds plum tomatoes, halved, seeded, chopped

6 ounces fresh soft goat cheese (such as Montrachet), coarsely crumbled
15 large garlic cloves, very thinly sliced
1½ cups thinly sliced fresh basil leaves (about 2 bunches)

Preheat broiler. Arrange eggplant slices on large baking sheet. Brush oil over both sides of eggplant. Season with salt and pepper. Broil until eggplant is tender and begins to brown, turning occasionally, about 6 minutes. Cool.

Place 2 large baking sheets in oven on separate racks and preheat to 500°F. Sprinkle 1 cup mozzarella cheese over each Boboli crust. Top with eggplant slices, chopped tomatoes, goat cheese, garlic slices and fresh basil. Sprinkle remaining mozzarella cheese over pizzas. Transfer Bobolis to preheated baking sheets in oven. Bake until cheeses melt and pizza edges are brown and crisp, about 12 minutes. Transfer to work surface. Let stand 10 minutes. Cut into wedges. Reassemble on platter and serve.

Vegetarian Pizza

6 servings

Sauce
2 tablespoons olive oil
1 large onion, chopped
1 large tomato, peeled, seeded, chopped
3 large garlic cloves, minced
¼ cup chopped fresh basil

Pizza
Cornmeal
1 1-pound loaf purchased frozen bread dough, thawed
1¾ cups grated provolone cheese (about 7 ounces)
¾ cup grated Parmesan cheese (about 3 ounces)
¼ cup chopped fresh basil

For sauce: Heat oil in heavy small skillet over medium heat. Add onion and sauté until translucent, about 6 minutes. Add tomato and garlic and cook until liquid evaporates, stirring occasionally, about 10 minutes. Mix in basil. Season to taste with salt and pepper. (*Can be prepared 1 day ahead. Refrigerate.*)

For pizza: Prepare barbecue (medium-high heat). Place pizza stone on grill and heat 5 minutes. Sprinkle rimless cookie sheet with cornmeal. Roll dough out on floured surface to 11-inch round. Transfer to prepared cookie sheet. Spread sauce over, leaving ½-inch border. Top with cheeses. Slide pizza onto stone on grill. Cover barbecue. Cook pizza until crust is crisp and cheeses melt, about 10 minutes. Sprinkle with basil and serve.

Shallot and Garlic Pizza with Two Cheeses

Ricotta salata and Romano are the cheeses on this innovative pie, which is topped with a fresh tomato and parsley salad.

Makes 1 pizza

Dough
- 1 cup warm water (105°F to 115°F)
- 1½ cups bread flour
- 1 cup all purpose flour
- 1 0.6-ounce cake fresh yeast, crumbled

- ½ cup semolina flour*
- 1 teaspoon salt
- 2 tablespoons olive oil

Topping
- 3 tablespoons olive oil
- 4 large shallots, thinly sliced
- 4 large garlic cloves, thinly sliced
- 2 tablespoons chopped fresh Italian parsley

Salad
- 4 large plum tomatoes (about 12 ounces total), seeded, chopped
- ¼ cup grated Romano cheese (about 1½ ounces)
- ½ cup chopped fresh Italian parsley
- ¼ cup olive oil
- 1 tablespoon balsamic vinegar or red wine vinegar

- ⅔ cup ricotta salata** or feta cheese, crumbled (about 2 ounces)
- ⅔ cup grated Romano cheese (about 3 ounces)

For dough: Combine 1 cup warm water, bread flour, ½ cup all purpose flour and crumbled yeast cake in large bowl. Cover dough and let stand at room temperature for 30 minutes.

Combine ½ cup semolina flour and 1 teaspoon salt and sprinkle onto work surface. Turn out dough and knead in semolina mixture. Drizzle with 2 tablespoons olive oil and knead in oil. Knead in remaining ½ cup all purpose flour. Continue to knead dough until smooth (dough will be soft, but not sticky), approximately 6 minutes.

Lightly oil large bowl. Add dough, turning to coat entire surface. Cover dough and let stand at room temperature until almost doubled, about 1 hour.

Punch dough down. Cover dough and refrigerate overnight.

Remove dough from refrigerator and let stand at room temperature until doubled, approximately 4 hours.

For topping: Heat 3 tablespoons olive oil in heavy medium skillet over medium heat. Add sliced shallots and sliced garlic cloves and sauté until tender, about 3 minutes. Remove from heat. Add 2 tablespoons chopped fresh Italian parsley. Set shallot mixture aside.

For salad: Combine chopped plum tomatoes, ¼ cup grated Romano cheese, chopped fresh parsley, olive oil and balsamic vinegar in large bowl. Season salad to taste with salt and pepper.

Place pizza stone in oven and preheat oven to 425°F. Generously flour rimless cookie sheet or pizza paddle. Roll dough out on lightly floured surface to 11-inch round. Transfer round to prepared cookie sheet or paddle. Sprinkle crumbled ricotta salata and ⅔ cup grated Romano cheese over top of dough, leaving ¾-inch border. Dot with shallot mixture. Slide pizza off cookie sheet or paddle and onto stone. Bake until crust is golden brown and cheeses melt, about 20 minutes. Top pizza with salad and serve immediately.

*Available at Italian markets and some specialty foods stores.
**Dried, salted ricotta available at cheese shops, Italian markets and some specialty foods stores.

Gouda and Red Salad Pizza

4 servings

1 medium radicchio head, thinly sliced

½ red onion, thinly sliced

½ large red bell pepper, thinly sliced

2 large plum tomatoes, seeded, thinly sliced

1 large red jalapeño chili, seeded, minced

2½ tablespoons balsamic vinegar or red wine vinegar

2 tablespoons olive oil

¾ teaspoon salt

½ teaspoon pepper

¼ eteaspoon sugar

2½ cups firmly packed shredded Gouda cheese (about 10 ounces)

1 16-ounce Boboli (baked cheese pizza crust)

Toss first 10 ingredients together in large bowl. Marinate until juices begin to accumulate in bowl, tossing occasionally, about 45 minutes.

Meanwhile, position rack in center of oven and preheat to 500°F. Place heavy large cookie sheet on rack and heat 30 minutes.

Drain vegetables well. Mix in 1 cup Gouda. Spread 1 cup of remaining Gouda over Boboli crust. Cover with vegetable mixture, spreading evenly. Top with remaining ½ cup Gouda. Transfer pizza to heated cookie sheet. Bake until cheese melts and edges of crust are crisp, about 12 minutes. Transfer to platter. Let stand 5 minutes before serving.

Sausage and Pepperoni Pizza "Pie"

This pie uses pizza toppings as a filling. Serve it with a tossed green salad.

6 servings

1 pound Italian sausage

1 15-ounce package refrigerated ready pie crusts

1 teaspoon all purpose flour

1 8-ounce package sliced mozzarella cheese

2 cups purchased spaghetti sauce

1 cup shredded Monterey Jack cheese (about 4 ounces)

3 ounces thinly sliced pepperoni

½ cup pimiento-stuffed green olives, sliced

Preheat oven to 425°F. Fry sausage in heavy medium skillet over medium heat until cooked through, turning occasionally. Drain. Dice sausage.

Dust 1 side of 1 crust with 1 teaspoon flour. Gently transfer crust to 9-inch-diameter pie pan, floured side down. Press into pan. Arrange half of mozzarella over bottom of crust. Spread ½ cup spaghetti sauce over mozzarella. Sprinkle half of Jack cheese atop sauce. Drizzle ½ cup spaghetti sauce over cheese. Top with half of pepperoni and half of sausage. Repeat layering with remaining mozzarella, ½ cup spaghetti sauce, remaining Jack cheese, pepperoni and sausage. Sprinkle with olives and drizzle with remaining ½ cup spaghetti sauce. Top with remaining pie crust. Pinch edges of crust together to seal. Crimp edges to make decorative border. Bake until golden brown, about 40 minutes. Let pie stand for about 30 minutes before serving.

Boboli Pizza with Garlic, Peppers and Goat Cheese

2 to 4 servings

¼ cup olive oil
1 large red onion, thinly sliced
6 large garlic cloves, thinly sliced
½ large red bell pepper, thinly sliced
½ large yellow or green bell pepper, thinly sliced
¼ teaspoon dried crushed red pepper

1 16-ounce Boboli (baked cheese pizza crust)
5 ounces soft goat cheese (such as Montrachet), crumbled
1 tablespoon fresh thyme leaves or 1 teaspoon dried, crumbled

Preheat oven to 450°F. Heat olive oil in heavy large skillet over medium-low heat. Add sliced onion and garlic and sauté until very soft, about 20 minutes. Add sliced bell peppers and sauté 5 minutes. Mix in dried crushed red pepper. Season mixture with salt and pepper.

Place Boboli on pizza pan or cookie sheet. Tip skillet so oil accumulates at one side. Brush Boboli with oil in skillet. Top with onion-pepper mixture. Sprinkle with cheese and thyme. Bake until cheese melts, about 12 minutes. Cut pizza into wedges and serve immediately.

 *Sandwiches*

Grilled Eggplant and Fontina Sandwiches

Serve hot corn on the cob as an easy accompaniment, then top off the meal with sliced fresh peaches and a plate of sugar cookies.

4 servings

½ cup olive oil
3 large garlic cloves, minced
1 large long eggplant (about 1½ pounds)

4 sourdough rolls (or any large crusty rolls), split horizontally

6 ounces Fontina or mozzarella cheese, thinly sliced
2 ripe tomatoes, thinly sliced
Thinly sliced red onion
Fresh basil leaves

Combine oil and garlic in small bowl and let stand at room temperature at least 15 minutes. Slice unpeeled eggplant into ½-inch-thick rounds. Place rounds on rack. Sprinkle both sides of eggplant liberally with salt. Let drain at least 15 minutes. Rinse eggplant and dry with paper towels. Brush both sides of eggplant generously with garlic oil.

Prepare barbecue (medium heat). Grill eggplant until slightly charred on outside and tender inside, turning frequently and brushing with oil, about 15 minutes. Transfer to plate. Brush cut side of rolls with garlic oil. Grill rolls, cut side down, until toasted and warmed through. Dividing remaining ingredients evenly among sandwiches, place eggplant rounds, cheese, tomato slices and onion slices on bottom half of each roll. Top with fresh basil leaves and upper half of each roll and serve.

Sloppy Joes

Spoon this flavorful mixture over split, toasted kaiser rolls. Garnish the sandwiches with crisp shredded lettuce. To complete the menu, top scoops of lemon ice cream with blueberry sauce and lots of fresh blueberries.

4 servings

1	tablespoon olive oil
1½	pounds ground beef
2	medium onions, chopped
1	green bell pepper, chopped
4	large garlic cloves, chopped
1½	tablespoons chili powder
2	28-ounce cans Italian plum tomatoes, drained, chopped

½	cup bottled chili sauce
½	cup canned beef broth
2	teaspoons red wine vinegar
1½	teaspoons Worcestershire sauce
3	tablespoons chopped fresh parsley

Heat olive oil in heavy large skillet over high heat. Add beef and cook until beginning to lose pink color, breaking up with fork, about 5 minutes. Reduce heat to medium. Mix in onions, green bell pepper and garlic. Cook until vegetables begin to soften, stirring occasionally, about 5 minutes. Mix in chili powder and stir 1 minute. Add tomatoes, chili sauce, broth, vinegar and Worcestershire sauce. Cook until vegetables are tender and mixture is thick, stirring occasionally, about 20 minutes. Season to taste with salt and pepper. (*Can be prepared 1 day ahead. Cover and refrigerate. Rewarm over low heat before continuing.*) Mix in chopped fresh parsley and serve.

Ham and Chick-Pea Salad Hero Sandwiches

This marinated chick-pea and ham mixture is a terrific hearty sandwich filling. It can also be offered—minus the rolls—as a main-course salad on a bed of greens of your choice. If you're running short on time, substitute 3⅓ cups drained canned chick-peas for the cooked dried ones.

Makes 8 sandwiches

1½	cups dried chick-peas (garbanzo beans)
8	cups water
⅓	cup balsamic vinegar or ¼ cup red wine vinegar
⅓	cup olive oil
2	large red bell peppers
2	cups ½-inch-dice baked ham (about ¾ pound)

1	medium-size red onion, diced
¾	cup finely chopped fresh Italian parsley
2	teaspoons pepper
8	crusty French bread rolls, each about 6 inches long
3	medium tomatoes, sliced
1	bunch arugula, stems trimmed

Soak chick-peas overnight in large pot with enough cold water to cover by 3 inches. (Or, to quick-soak peas, place peas in large pot with enough cold water to cover by 3 inches and bring to boil. Remove pot from heat. Cover and let stand 1 hour.) Drain well.

Bring chick-peas and 8 cups water to boil in heavy large pot over medium heat. Reduce heat, cover partially and simmer 20 minutes. Add salt and cook chick-peas until just tender, stirring occasionally, about 30 minutes. Drain well. Transfer to large bowl. Pour vinegar and oil over chick-peas. Cool completely, stirring occasionally. (*Can be prepared 1 day ahead; refrigerate.*)

Char bell peppers over gas flame or in broiler until blackened on all sides. Wrap in paper bag and let stand 10 minutes to steam. Peel and seed. Rinse if necessary; pat dry. Cut into ½-inch dice. Add bell peppers and ham to chick-peas. Mix in onion, parsley and pepper. Adjust seasoning.

Halve rolls horizontally. Pull out centers, leaving ¾-inch shell. Spoon salad into bottom halves, stuffing as full as possible. Pour any remaining oil and vinegar in bowl over sandwiches. Top with tomato slices and arugula. Close sandwiches, pressing firmly with palm of hand to flatten slightly. Cover with plastic and let stand 1 hour at room temperature before serving.

Salami, Cheese and Sage Sandwiches

Makes 10 half-sandwiches

10 4 × 6-inch slices sourdough bread, ½ inch thick
2 tablespoons (about) water
2 tablespoons (about) olive oil
20 large fresh sage leaves
2 tablespoons (or more) butter

Mustard Butter (see recipe)
½ pound thinly sliced dry salami

15 paper-thin lemon slices
2 large tomatoes, cut into 10 thin slices each
½ pound sliced Swiss cheese
Mayonnaise
Lemon wedges and fresh sage leaves

Trim bread into 3½ × 5½-inch rectangles. Lightly brush 1 side of each bread slice with water, then with olive oil. Place 2 sage leaves on each slice near opposite corners. Melt 2 tablespoons butter in heavy large skillet over medium heat. Add 2 bread slices, sage side down, and fry until beginning to brown, about 1 minute. Transfer to work surface, cooked side down, pressing sage leaves in place if necessary. Repeat with remaining slices, adding more butter if necessary. (*Can be prepared 1 hour ahead. Wrap and store at room temperature.*)

Spread uncooked side of 5 bread slices with Mustard Butter. Layer on salami, lemon, tomato and Swiss cheese. Spread uncooked side of remaining 5 slices with mayonnaise side down atop sandwiches. Halve sandwiches diagonally. Garnish with lemon wedges and fresh sage leaves.

Mustard Butter

Makes about ½ cup

½ cup (1 stick) butter, room temperature

2 tablespoons Dijon mustard

Mix butter and mustard in small bowl. (*Can be prepared 2 days ahead. Refrigerate. Bring to room temperature before using.*)

4 ❦ Main Courses

When it comes to cooking, most of us concentrate our efforts on the main course, in terms of both time and expense, whether planning a meal for our family or guests. That's why here, in the heart of the book, we've compiled more than 50 recipes for everything from beef to lamb to chicken to seafood, many of them quick and simple to make, some of them a bit more challenging, the kind of dish you might prepare for company. So whether you're looking for something new to do with ground beef or an elegant idea for Saturday night's dinner party for eight, you'll be sure to come across just the right recipe here.

Dinner was never so easy as Meat Loaf Plus, a delicious, simple version of that popular "comfort food." If you're entertaining, try sophisticated Beef Tenderloin with Herb Crust and Cabernet Sauce, or wonderfully hearty Garlic and Rosemary Steak with Potato-Onion Cakes. If you're splurging on veal or lamb, consider Veal Chops with Artichoke, Tomato and Mushroom Sauce or Grilled Mongolian Lamb with Thai Curry Sauce, both impressive, intriguing dishes. And now that pork is lighter and leaner, we can afford to indulge in the likes of Roast Pork with Spicy Lima Bean Stew and Wilted Greens more often.

Those two popular staples, poultry and seafood, turn up here dressed up and dressed down, in quick-to-cook recipes like Turkey Cutlets with Paprika Cream Sauce, Baked Fish with Tomatoes and Garlic and more exotic variations on the theme, among them Island Chicken with Ginger-Lime Sauce, and Shrimp and Mushrooms in Spicy Black Bean Oyster Sauce.

At the end of the chapter there is a selection of egg, cheese and vegetable main courses, just what you're looking for if you've been eating less red meat lately. You certainly won't miss it in Vegetable Lasagne with Tomato Sauce—colorful carrot, spinach and eggplant layers topped with cheese and served with a do-ahead tomato sauce.

 *Beef*

Roast Sirloin of Beef

8 servings

2 tablespoons olive oil
1 6-pound beef rib roast (loin end), well trimmed

1 leek, coarsely chopped
1 celery stalk, coarsely chopped
1 small carrot, coarsely chopped

½ onion, coarsely chopped
3 fresh parsley stems
1 bay leaf
½ teaspoon dried thyme, crumbled
1 cup beef stock or canned broth

Preheat oven to 450°F. Heat oil in heavy large skillet over high heat. Season beef rib roast with salt and pepper. Add to skillet and brown on all sides, about 12 minutes. Transfer beef to roasting pan and roast for 20 minutes, basting occasionally with pan drippings. Reduce oven temperature to 350°F and continue roasting until thermometer inserted in thickest part of beef registers 120°F for rare, approximately 55 minutes.

Meanwhile, transfer 3 tablespoons beef drippings from roasting pan to heavy large skillet. Add vegetables and herbs and sauté over medium heat until brown, about 25 minutes. Add stock and boil 4 minutes. Set aside.

Transfer beef to heated platter to let stand 20 minutes. Degrease roasting pan juices. Add reserved stock mixture and bring to boil, scraping up any browned bits. Strain sauce. Carve roast and serve with sauce.

Italian Meat Loaf

4 to 6 servings

2 slices rye bread
2 slices firm white bread
1 cup water
1 pound lean ground beef
1 medium onion, finely chopped
1 egg, beaten to blend
3 tablespoons grated Parmesan cheese

2 tablespoons minced fresh parsley
1 teaspoon salt
¼ teaspoon pepper

1 8-ounce can tomato sauce
1 teaspoon dried oregano, crumbled

Grease 9 × 5-inch loaf pan. Place rye and white breads in large bowl. Pour 1 cup water over. Let soak 5 minutes. Drain off any excess water. Mash bread finely with fork. Add ground beef, onion, egg, Parmesan, parsley, salt and pepper and mix well. Transfer to prepared dish. (*Can be prepared 6 hours ahead. Chill.*)

Preheat oven to 375°F. Bake meat loaf 30 minutes. Pour tomato sauce over. Sprinkle with oregano. Bake 20 more minutes. Let stand 5 minutes.

Garlic and Rosemary Steak with Potato-Onion Cakes

6 servings

Steak
- ½ cup olive oil
- ½ cup soy sauce
- ¼ cup balsamic vinegar or red wine vinegar
- 8 large garlic cloves, minced
- 4 teaspoons dried rosemary, crumbled
- 1 2-inch-thick boneless top sirloin steak (about 3½ pounds)

Peppers and Onions
- ⅓ cup olive oil
- 2 large onions, cut into 1-inch pieces
- 2 red bell peppers, cut into 1-inch pieces
- 1 green bell pepper, cut into 1-inch pieces
- ¾ teaspoon dried marjoram, crumbled
- ⅛ teaspoon dried crushed red pepper

Potato-Onion Cakes (see recipe)

For steak: Combine first 5 ingredients in glass baking dish. Add steak and turn to coat. Season with pepper. Cover and chill overnight, turning occasionally.

For peppers and onions: Heat oil in heavy large skillet over medium-high heat. Add onions and sauté 4 minutes. Add peppers and sauté until beginning to soften, about 8 minutes. Add marjoram and dried red pepper. Season to taste with salt and pepper and stir 2 minutes. Remove from heat.

Bring steak to room temperature. Preheat broiler 5 minutes. Remove steak from marinade; pat dry. Transfer marinade to heavy small saucepan. Broil steak to desired degree of doneness, about 10 minutes per side for rare (meat thermometer will register 125°F for rare). Transfer to platter. Let stand 10 minutes.

Meanwhile, reheat bell peppers and onions. Bring marinade to boil.

Thinly slice steak across grain. Arrange on platter. Surround with Potato-Onion Cakes, peppers and onions. Serve, passing marinade separately.

Potato-Onion Cakes

Makes about 14

- 3 pounds white potatoes (about 6 large)
- 12 green onions (white and green parts), chopped
- 2 eggs
- 2 teaspoons ground cumin
- 3 tablespoons (about) olive oil

Boil potatoes in large pot of water just until centers can be pierced with sharp knife, about 20 minutes. Drain. Cover potatoes and refrigerate until well chilled. (*Can be prepared 1 day ahead.*)

Peel potatoes. Using hand grater, coarsely grate potatoes into large bowl. Gently mix in green onions. Season to taste with salt and pepper. Beat eggs with cumin and gently mix into potato mixture. Form potatoes into 2½-inch-diameter cakes (about 1 inch thick). Cover and refrigerate until ready to cook. (*Can be prepared up to 6 hours ahead.*)

Heat 2 tablespoons oil in heavy large skillet over medium-high heat. Add potato cakes in batches and fry until golden brown, about 8 minutes per side, adding more oil as necessary. Serve immediately.

Calf's Liver with Bacon and Garlic

You can vary the amount of garlic here to suit your own taste, of course.

4 servings

3 bacon slices
4 calf's liver slices (4 ounces each)
   All purpose flour

1 tablespoon butter
8 garlic cloves, thinly sliced
   Chopped fresh parsley

Cook bacon in heavy large skillet over medium heat until crisp. Transfer bacon to paper towel to drain. Crumble bacon. Discard all but 1 tablespoon drippings from skillet. Season liver with salt and pepper. Dredge in flour; shake off excess. Melt butter in same skillet over high heat. Add liver and cook to desired doneness, about 1 minute per side for medium. Transfer liver to plates. Add garlic to skillet and cook until golden, stirring constantly, about 2 minutes. Spoon garlic over liver. Sprinkle with crumbled bacon and parsley and serve.

Beef Tenderloin with Herb Crust and Cabernet Sauce

4 servings

Herb Crust
2¼ cups fresh egg-bread breadcrumbs
   2 cups chopped fresh parsley
   3 tablespoons chopped fresh thyme
      or 2 teaspoons dried, crumbled
   ½ cup (1 stick) unsalted butter,
      melted

Sauce
   2 bottles Cabernet Sauvignon wine
   1 bottle tawny Port
   4 cups beef stock or canned
      unsalted broth

Beef and Potatoes
   4 medium baking potatoes
   ¾ cup whipping cream
   4 tablespoons olive oil
      Ground nutmeg

   4 1-inch-thick beef tenderloin
      steaks (about 8 ounces each)

   ¼ cup (½ stick) unsalted butter

For herb crust: Combine breadcrumbs with herbs. Pour butter over and mix well. Season with salt and pepper.

For sauce: Pour red wine, Port and stock into heavy large pot. Bring to simmer over medium-high heat. Continue to simmer until reduced to 1 cup, about 1 hour 45 minutes. (*Can be prepared 2 days ahead. Cover sauce and crust mixture separately and refrigerate.*)

For beef and potatoes: Bring large saucepan of salted water to boil. Add potatoes and cook until tender. Drain potatoes and return to pan. Cook over low heat until dry, about 3 minutes. Peel warm potatoes; press through ricer into bowl. Using electric mixer, add cream and 2 tablespoons oil and beat until potatoes are smooth. Season with salt and nutmeg. Place potatoes in pastry bag fitted with ⅜-inch (no. 8) plain tip.

Season steaks with salt and pepper. Heat remaining 2 tablespoons oil in heavy large skillet over high heat. Brown steaks about 4 minutes per side. Remove from heat and let stand 20 minutes.

Preheat broiler. Spread breadcrumb mixture on top of steaks, pressing to adhere. Broil until breadcrumbs are golden brown. Reduce oven to 450°F. Place steaks on ovenproof plates. Pipe potatoes onto plates. Transfer to oven and bake until potatoes and steaks are heated through, about 10 minutes. Heat sauce in medium saucepan. Whisk in butter. Nap steaks with sauce and serve.

Fiesta Fajitas

Set out baskets of flour tortillas and bowls of guacamole and Pico de Gallo so guests can assemble their own fajitas.

24 servings

4½ cups fresh lime juice (about 25 large limes)
4½ cups soy sauce
4½ cups Worcestershire sauce
9 pounds beef skirt steaks, fat trimmed, cut in half crosswise
5 green bell peppers, quartered

5 red bell peppers, quartered
4½ onions, cut into ½-inch-thick rounds

72 (about) warm flour tortillas
Easy Guacamole (see recipe)
Pico de Gallo (see recipe)

Place lime juice in large bowl. Gradually whisk in soy and Worcestershire sauces. Transfer to large roasting pan. Add steaks, bell peppers and onions and turn to coat. Cover tightly. Refrigerate 2 hours, turning steaks occasionally.

Prepare barbecue (medium-high heat). Drain steaks, bell peppers and onions. Place on grill. Cook until steaks are medium-rare and bell peppers and onions are tender and lightly charred, turning steaks, bell peppers and onions occasionally, about 10 minutes.

Transfer steaks, bell peppers and onions to cutting board. Cut steaks diagonally across grain into thin slices. Cut bell peppers into strips. Halve onions to separate rings. Mound steak, bell peppers and onions on platter. Serve with warm flour tortillas, guacamole and Pico de Gallo.

Easy Guacamole

This recipe makes enough to serve as a dip with tortilla chips and as a topping to go with the fajitas.

Makes about 12 cups

15 ripe avocados, halved, pitted, peeled
1½ cups purchased medium-hot salsa

2 tablespoons buttermilk ranch-style salad dressing mix
Tortilla chips

Place avocados in large bowl and mash coarsely. Stir in salsa and buttermilk dressing mix. (*Can be prepared 2 hours ahead. Press plastic wrap onto surface of guacamole and refrigerate.*) Serve guacamole with tortilla chips.

Pico de Gallo

A spicy fresh salsa best eaten within a few hours of preparation.

Makes about 10 cups

6 cups drained chopped tomatoes (about 6 large)
3 medium onions, finely chopped

1½ cups chopped fresh cilantro
6 jalapeño chilies, seeded, finely chopped

Mix all ingredients in large bowl. Season to taste with salt and pepper. (*Can be prepared 3 hours ahead. Cover and let stand at room temperature.*)

Skirt Steak with Shallots

2 servings

1 12-ounce skirt steak

5 tablespoons unsalted butter

2 large shallots, minced

¼ cup chopped fresh parsley

To butterfly steak, cut crosswise in half. Starting at 1 long side, halve steak horizontally to within ¼ inch of opposite long side. Open as for book; press to flatten. Repeat with second steak piece.

Melt 1 tablespoon butter in heavy large skillet. Season steaks with salt and pepper. Add 1 steak to skillet and cook to desired doneness, about 1½ minutes per side for medium-rare. Transfer to platter. Tent with foil to keep warm. Repeat cooking process with second steak. Transfer to platter. Melt remaining 4 tablespoons butter in same skillet. Add shallots and sauté 3 minutes. Mix in parsley. Spoon sauce over steaks.

Beef Stroganoff

4 servings

2 cups beef stock or canned broth

1 pound beef fillet, cut into 2 × 1 × ¼-inch slices

2 tablespoons (¼ stick) unsalted butter

3 tablespoons vegetable oil

1 small onion, sliced

½ red bell pepper, thinly sliced

½ yellow bell pepper, thinly sliced

½ cup chopped dill pickles

¼ cup brandy

2 cups whipping cream

5 teaspoons Hungarian sweet paprika

12 ounces fettuccine

1 tablespoon fresh lemon juice

6 drops hot pepper sauce (such as Tabasco)

Sour cream

2 tablespoons chopped fresh parsley

Boil beef stock in heavy medium saucepan until reduced to ½ cup, about 15 minutes. Set stock aside.

Season beef with salt and pepper. Melt butter in heavy large skillet over high heat. Add beef and sauté to desired doneness, about 4 minutes for medium. Transfer beef slices to bowl.

Heat oil in heavy large deep skillet over high heat. Add onion, bell peppers and pickles and sauté 3 minutes. Remove skillet from heat. Add brandy and ignite with match. When flames subside, return skillet to heat. Add reduced stock, cream and paprika. Simmer until reduced to sauce consistency, stirring occasionally, approximately 15 minutes.

Meanwhile, cook fettuccine in large pot of boiling salted water until just tender but still firm to bite, stirring occasionally. Drain thoroughly.

Add beef, lemon juice and hot pepper sauce to cream sauce. Season with salt and pepper. Stir mixture until heated.

Divide fettucine among plates. Spoon beef and sauce over. Garnish with sour cream and chopped fresh parsley.

Beef Brisket Braised with Dried Fruit, Yams and Carrots

This can be prepared up to one day ahead.

8 servings

3 tablespoons vegetable oil
3 medium onions, chopped
4 large garlic cloves, chopped
1 teaspoon paprika
½ teaspoon ground allspice
¼ teaspoon dried crushed red pepper
3½ cups chicken stock or canned broth
1½ cups dry red wine
3 bay leaves

1 4-pound boneless first-cut beef brisket
Paprika
1 6-ounce package dried apricots
1½ cups pitted prunes

3 pounds yams, peeled, cut into 1½-inch pieces
6 large carrots, peeled, cut into 1½-inch pieces
Minced fresh parsley

Preheat oven to 325°F. Heat oil in heavy large pot or Dutch oven over medium-high heat. Add onions and garlic and cook until beginning to brown, stirring frequently, about 15 minutes. Add 1 teaspoon paprika, allspice and crushed red pepper and stir 20 seconds. Add chicken stock, wine and bay leaves. Boil 10 minutes to blend flavors.

Sprinkle brisket with paprika and rub in. Add brisket to pot, fat side up. Add dried apricots and pitted prunes. Cover and bake 1½ hours.

Add yams and carrots to pot. Cover and cook until brisket is very tender, about 2½ hours longer. Remove from oven and let stand 20 minutes. Remove brisket from pot and slice thinly across grain. Arrange on platter. Degrease pan juices. Spoon pan juices over meat. Arrange fruit and vegetables around meat. Garnish with minced fresh parsley and serve. (*Can be prepared 2 days ahead. Cover and refrigerate before slicing meat. To serve, remove meat from pot and slice thinly across grain. Remove any solid fat from sauce. Return sliced meat to pot. Place pot in 325°F oven and bake until heated through, 30 minutes.*)

Meat Loaf Plus

The "plus" in this delicious dish? Chopped green olives, savory onion soup mix and a dash of red wine.

4 servings

1 pound plus 2 ounces ground beef
1 cup herbed seasoned stuffing
2 eggs, beaten to blend
½ cup dry red wine

10 pimiento-stuffed green olives, chopped
3 tablespoons minced fresh parsley
1 envelope onion soup mix
2 garlic cloves, minced

Preheat oven to 350°F. Combine all ingredients in large bowl. Season with salt and pepper. Mix thoroughly. Transfer mixture to greased 8½ × 4½-inch loaf pan. Bake until meat loaf shrinks from sides of pan and top is brown, about 1 hour. Turn out onto platter and serve.

Veal

Veal Piccata with Capers and Pine Nuts

2 servings

2 bacon slices, chopped
6 ounces veal scallops (about
  6 scallops), pounded very thin
  All purpose flour (for dredging)
4 tablespoons (½ stick) unsalted
  butter

½ cup dry white wine
3 tablespoons toasted pine nuts
1 tablespoon drained capers
2 teaspoons minced fresh sage or
  ½ teaspoon dried rubbed sage
  Fresh sage leaves (optional)

Cook bacon in heavy large skillet over medium-high heat until crisp. Transfer to bowl using slotted spoon. Season veal with salt and pepper. Dredge in flour; shake off excess. Add 1 tablespoon butter to pan drippings in skillet and melt over medium-high heat. Add veal and sauté until just cooked through, about 1 minute per side. Divide veal between 2 plates; tent with foil to keep warm. Add wine to same skillet and bring to boil, scraping up any browned bits. Boil until liquid is reduced to 3 tablespoons, about 2 minutes. Whisk in remaining 3 tablespoons butter. Mix in pine nuts, capers, minced sage and bacon. Season with pepper. Spoon sauce over veal. Garnish with sage leaves and serve.

Veal Chops with Roquefort Sauce

4 servings

3 cups chicken stock or canned
  low-salt broth
2 cups beef stock or canned
  unsalted broth
2 shallots, minced

4 small new potatoes, quartered

8 tablespoons (1 stick) unsalted
  butter
1 carrot, peeled, cut into
  matchstick-size strips

1 leek (white and pale green parts
  only), cut into matchstick-size
  strips
4 1-inch-thick veal loin chops
  (about 6 ounces each)
4 thin slices Roquefort cheese
  (about 2 ounces)
1½ ounces Roquefort cheese,
  crumbled

Minced fresh chives

Boil both stocks with shallots in heavy medium saucepan until reduced to ¾ cup, about 45 minutes. (*Can be prepared 1 day ahead. Cover and refrigerate.*)

Preheat oven to 400°F. Butter large baking sheet. Arrange potatoes on baking sheet. Roast potatoes until golden brown, about 40 minutes.

Meanwhile, melt 1 tablespoon butter in heavy medium skillet over medium heat. Add carrot and sauté 3 minutes. Add leek and sauté 2 minutes. Season with salt and pepper to taste. Set aside. Melt 1 tablespoon butter in heavy large skillet over medium-high heat. Season veal with salt and pepper. Add to skillet and cook to desired doneness, about 4 minutes per side for medium-rare. Transfer to plates; do not clean skillet. Top each chop with slice of Roquefort. Tent with foil to keep warm. Add reduced stock mixture to skillet veal was cooked in and

bring to boil, scraping up any browned bits. Whisk in crumbled Roquefort cheese. Add remaining 6 tablespoons butter and whisk just until melted.

Spoon sauce over veal. Cook carrots and leeks over medium-high heat until heated through. Mound atop veal. Surround with potatoes. Sprinkle with chives.

Veal Chops with Artichoke, Tomato and Mushroom Sauce

4 servings

Sauce
- ¼ cup plus 2 tablespoons Madeira wine
- 2 cups chicken stock or canned low-salt broth
- 1 cup beef stock or canned unsalted broth

Vegetables and Veal
- 2 artichokes
- 1 lemon, cut in half

- 8 tablespoons (1 stick) butter
- ¾ pound mushrooms, quartered
- 2 tablespoons olive oil
- 4 veal chops (about 12 ounces each)
  All purpose flour

- 2 large tomatoes, peeled, seeded, cut into matchstick-size strips
- 1 tablespoon minced fresh parsley
- 1 tablespoon chopped fresh chives
- 1 teaspoon chopped fresh thyme or ¼ teaspoon dried, crumbled

For sauce: Boil ¼ cup Madeira in heavy medium saucepan until reduced by half. Add both stocks and continue to boil until reduced to ½ cup, about 20 minutes. (*Can be prepared 2 days ahead. Cover and refrigerate.*)

For vegetables and veal: Cut stem off artichokes and rub exposed area with cut side of lemon. Starting at base, bend back each dark green leaf and snap off. Cut off tight cone of tender yellow leaves above heart of artichokes. Rub exposed areas with lemon. Bring medium saucepan of salted water to boil. Add artichoke hearts and squeeze in remaining lemon juice. Simmer until artichokes are tender, about 15 minutes. Drain. Scoop out and discard chokes. Cut artichoke hearts into matchstick-size strips.

Melt 2 tablespoons butter in heavy large skillet over medium heat. Add mushrooms and sauté until golden brown, about 12 minutes. Transfer to bowl. Heat oil in same skillet. Season veal with salt and pepper. Dredge in flour, tapping off excess. Cook veal until golden brown and just cooked through, about 7 minutes per side. Place on plates and keep warm.

Add remaining 2 tablespoons Madeira to skillet and bring to boil, scraping up any browned bits. Stir in reduced stock mixture. Gradually whisk in remaining 6 tablespoons butter. Add mushrooms, artichokes and tomatoes. Cook until vegetables are warm. Stir in parsley, chives and thyme. Season to taste with pepper. Spoon sauce and vegetables over veal.

2 servings

All purpose flour
6 ounces veal scallops
2 tablespoons (¼ stick) butter

5 tablespoons whipping cream
2 tablespoons (or more) freshly
 grated horseradish or 2 teaspoons
 prepared horseradish

¼ cup peeled seeded diced tomato
2 teaspoons minced fresh parsley
2 teaspoons minced fresh chives

Season flour with salt and white pepper. Dredge veal in flour; shake off excess. Melt butter in heavy large skillet over high heat. Add veal and cook until just tender, about 2 minutes per side. Divide veal between plates; tent with foil to keep warm. Wipe out skillet.

Add cream and 2 tablespoons horseradish to same skillet and boil until liquid is reduced by half, about 2 minutes. Taste, adding more horseradish if desired. Add tomato, parsley and chives and stir to heat through. Spoon cream sauce over veal and serve immediately.

 # Lamb

Braised Lamb in Pomegranate Sauce

Order the lamb shoulder from your butcher, and purchase the pomegranate juice at a Middle Eastern market or natural foods store. Begin preparing this richly flavored main course one day ahead.

8 servings

¼ cup olive oil
1 pound lamb neck bones
1 7- to 7½-pound lamb shoulder,
 boned (bones reserved), well
 trimmed, rolled, tied
 All purpose flour

2 medium onions, chopped
10 large garlic cloves
2 cups chicken stock or canned
 broth
1 cup dry red wine
1 cup unsweetened pomegranate
 juice

2 tablespoons tomato paste
2 tablespoons firmly packed golden
 brown sugar
1 tablespoon dried oregano,
 crumbled
1 teaspoon ground cinnamon
¾ teaspoon ground allspice
1½ tablespoons margarine
1½ tablespoons all purpose flour
 Chopped fresh parsley

Position rack in lowest third of oven and preheat to 325°F. Heat oil in heavy large pot or Dutch oven over high heat. Add lamb neck bones and reserved shoulder bones and cook until brown, turning frequently, about 15 minutes. Transfer bones to plate. Season lamb with salt and pepper and dredge thoroughly in flour. Add to pot and cook until brown on all sides, about 10 minutes. Transfer lamb to plate with bones.

Add onions and garlic to pot and cook until onions are just golden brown, scraping up browned bits on bottom, about 5 minutes. Return lamb to pot.

Arrange bones around lamb. Add chicken stock and next 7 ingredients. Stir to blend. Bring liquids to boil. Baste top of lamb. Cover tightly. Bake in oven until lamb is tender when pierced with long sharp knife, turning once, about 2¼ hours. Cool. Cover and refrigerate overnight.

Preheat oven to 325°F. Remove fat from surface of lamb and cooking liquid. Transfer lamb to platter. Remove string from lamb. Cut into ½-inch-thick slices. Arrange slices in shallow baking dish.

Bring pan juices to boil. Remove bones and discard. Strain pan juices, pressing hard on solids to extract as much liquid as possible. Melt margarine in same pot over medium heat. Add 1½ tablespoons flour and stir until mixture begins to brown, about 2 minutes. Whisk in pan juices and boil until sauce is reduced to 2 cups, about 15 minutes. Season to taste with salt and pepper. Pour sauce over lamb. Cover with foil and bake until lamb is heated through, about 25 minutes. Arrange lamb slices on platter. Spoon sauce over lamb. Garnish with chopped parsley and serve.

Roast Leg of Lamb with Pesto, Radicchio and Shallots

Using purchased pesto sauce makes this recipe a snap. For best flavor, marinate the lamb overnight. A simple green salad is an easy accompaniment.

6 servings

1 5- to 6-pound leg of lamb
1 7- to 8-ounce package purchased pesto sauce

8 ounces shallots, peeled
2 medium heads radicchio, each cut into 3 wedges (do not core)
Fresh basil sprigs

Cut excess fat from leg of lamb, leaving thin layer. Set lamb in medium roasting pan. Make several slits in lamb and spoon some pesto into each. Rub remaining pesto into lamb. Cover lamb and let stand 2 hours at room temperature or refrigerate overnight.

Preheat oven to 350°F. Roast lamb 30 minutes. Add shallots to pan, turning to coat in pan juices. Roast 45 minutes. Add radicchio, turning to coat in juices. Continue roasting until thermometer inserted into thickest part of meat registers 140°F for medium-rare, about 45 minutes longer. Remove from oven and let stand 15 minutes. Transfer lamb, shallots and radicchio to platter. Garnish with fresh basil sprigs and serve immediately.

Mint-marinated Leg of Lamb

Sautéed zucchini or spinach makes a delicious accompaniment. Baklava from a local Middle Eastern market is the ideal sweet.

8 servings

½ cup olive oil
½ cup dry red wine
¼ cup packed minced fresh mint
4 large garlic cloves, minced
2 bay leaves, crumbled

1 5-pound leg of lamb, boned, butterflied

Fresh mint sprigs

Mix first 5 ingredients in large glass baking dish. Season with generous amount of pepper. Add lamb, turning to coat. Cover and refrigerate overnight.

Preheat oven to 450°F. Drain lamb and transfer to large roasting pan. Season both sides with salt and generous amount of pepper. Arrange fat side down in pan. Roast 15 minutes. Reduce oven temperature to 375°F and continue roasting until thermometer inserted in thickest part of lamb registers 130°F for rare, about 20 minutes. Let stand 10 minutes. Cut into slices. Arrange on platter. Garnish with mint sprigs and serve.

Grilled Mongolian Lamb with Thai Curry Sauce

Serve this delectable lamb with purchased chutney, or try the Tropical Mint Chutney here.

4 servings

Sauce

    1 tablespoon peanut oil
  ¼ cup chopped onion
    3 tablespoons chopped celery
    2 tablespoons chopped carrot
    1 tablespoon curry powder
    3 cups chicken stock or canned
       low-salt broth
    1 cup beef stock or canned unsalted
       broth
    1 cup whipping cream
  ½ cup canned coconut milk*

Lamb

    1 cup soy sauce
  ½ cup sugar
    3 large garlic cloves, chopped
    2 teaspoons chili paste with
       garlic**
    1 2-inch piece fresh ginger, minced
    2 1¼-pound racks of lamb,
       trimmed

    3 large fresh basil leaves, thinly
       sliced
       Tropical Mint Chutney (see
       recipe)

For sauce: Heat oil in heavy large saucepan over medium heat. Add onion, celery and carrot. Sauté until vegetables are golden brown and tender, about 5 minutes. Stir in curry and cook 2 minutes. Whisk in chicken and beef stocks. Boil over medium-high heat until reduced to 1 cup, about 30 minutes. Add cream and coconut milk. Reduce heat and simmer until reduced to 1¼ cups, about 15 minutes. (*Can be prepared 1 day ahead. Cover and refrigerate.*)

For lamb: Combine first 5 ingredients in medium bowl. Add lamb and turn to coat well. Marinate lamb for 1 hour.

Prepare barbecue (medium-high heat) or preheat broiler. Drain lamb. Grill or broil about 4 minutes per side for rare. Let rest 10 minutes.

Reheat sauce over medium heat. Stir in basil. Cut lamb into individual ribs. Divide among plates. Nap with sauce and serve with chutney.

  *Available at Indian, Southeast Asian or Latin American markets and some supermarkets.
  **Available at oriental markets and in the oriental section of some supermarkets.

Tropical Mint Chutney

The perfect partner for lamb, pork or chicken. You can also use it as a quick and easy way to spice up steamed rice; stir in the chutney just before serving.

Makes about 2½ cups

    1 cup raspberry or other fruit-
       flavored vinegar
  ½ cup red wine vinegar
    2 cups dry white wine
    1 cup diced peeled pineapple
    1 cup diced apple
  ⅔ cup diced peeled papaya
  ⅔ cup diced peeled mango
  ⅔ cup diced peeled orange

    1 cup thinly sliced red or green
       bell pepper
  ½ cup thinly sliced yellow bell
       pepper
  ¼ cup plus 2 tablespoons honey
    6 whole peppercorns
    1 large bay leaf
    2 tablespoons minced fresh mint

Combine vinegars in heavy medium saucepan. Boil over medium heat until reduced to ½ cup, about 5 minutes. Add wine, fruit, bell peppers, honey, peppercorns and bay leaf. Cook until fruit is softened, about 5 minutes. Using slotted spoon, transfer fruit and bell peppers to small bowl. Simmer liquid until syrupy, about 8 minutes. Return fruit mixture to saucepan and cook over low heat until reduced to 2½ cups, about 20 minutes. Remove peppercorns and bay leaf. Transfer chutney to large bowl and cool. Stir in minced fresh mint. (*Chutney can be prepared 3 days ahead. Cover and refrigerate.*)

Pork

Roast Pork with Spicy Lima Bean Stew and Wilted Greens

This dish is both homey and modern at the same time. Begin preparation one day ahead. The jalapeño chilies give the lima beans a nice zip.

4 servings

Pork and Spicy Beans
- 1 cup dried lima beans
- 1 tablespoon olive oil
- 2½ pounds boneless pork butt, trimmed, tied
- 2 bacon slices, coarsely chopped
- 2 small carrots, cut into 3-inch pieces
- 2 stalks celery, cut into 3-inch pieces
- ½ onion, chopped
- 6 fresh thyme sprigs or 1 teaspoon dried, crumbled
- 4 garlic cloves, minced

- 1 to 2 jalapeño chilies, halved
- 1 bay leaf
- 3½ cups chicken stock or canned broth
- 1 tablespoon red wine vinegar

Greens
- 1 tablespoon olive oil
- ½ onion, thinly sliced
- 4 cups chopped kale leaves (about 4 ounces)
- 4 cups chopped mustard greens (about 4 ounces)
- 2 cups chopped seeded tomatoes
- 2 tablespoons red wine vinegar

For pork and spicy beans: Place lima beans in medium bowl. Cover with water. Soak overnight. Drain lima beans.

Preheat oven to 375°F. Heat olive oil in heavy large Dutch oven over high heat. Season pork with salt and pepper. Add to pan and brown on all sides, about 8 minutes. Remove pork and set aside. Pour off all but 1 tablespoon drippings from pan. Reduce heat to medium. Add chopped bacon and sauté 1 minute. Add carrots, celery, chopped onion, thyme sprigs, minced garlic, jalapeño chilies and bay leaf and sauté 3 minutes. Add lima beans, chicken stock and red wine vinegar to pan and bring mixture to boil. Remove from heat. Place pork atop bean mixture. Transfer to oven and roast until pork and lima beans are tender, about 1 hour. Remove pork from pan and let rest 10 minutes. Remove and discard jalapeño chilies.

For greens: Heat olive oil in heavy large skillet over medium-high heat. Add sliced onion and sauté 1 minute. Stir in chopped kale, chopped mustard greens, tomatoes and red wine vinegar. Cook until greens wilt, about 4 minutes. Season greens with salt and pepper.

Cut pork into ¼-inch-thick slices. Divide beans among plates and top with pork and greens. Serve immediately.

Sautéed Pork Tenderloin with Mango Sauce

2 servings

- 1 large mango, peeled
- 2 8-ounce pork tenderloins
- 1 tablespoon butter

- ¼ cup dry Sherry
- ½ cup chicken stock or canned broth
- Chopped fresh cilantro

Cut six 3-inch-long ½-inch-wide strips from mango. Remove pit. Chop remaining mango. Puree 1 cup chopped mango in blender or processor. Reserve any leftover chopped mango to garnish pork. Reserve puree for sauce.

Place pork on work surface. Butterfly by making lengthwise cut down 1 side

of meat, cutting ²⁄₃ through. Open meat as for book. Make another lengthwise cut down center of each cut side, cutting ⅓ through. Press to flatten. Season pork with pepper. Place mango strips lengthwise down center of meat. Fold meat in half, enclosing filling. Tie pork crosswise with string at 1-inch intervals to hold shape. (*Can be prepared 4 hours ahead. Cover and refrigerate.*)

Melt butter in heavy large skillet over medium heat. Add pork and sauté until golden brown on all sides and cooked through, about 15 minutes. Transfer to platter and tent with foil. Add Sherry to same skillet and cook 2 minutes. Whisk in stock and boil 1 minute. Stir in reserved mango puree. Cook until heated through, stirring occasionally. Divide sauce among plates. Slice pork and arrange atop sauce. Sprinkle with chopped fresh cilantro and any leftover chopped mango. Serve immediately.

Pork Tenderloin with Lima Bean-Tarragon Sauce

8 servings

Bean Sauce
- ½ cup dried baby lima beans
- 1 tablespoon olive oil
- 2 ounces tasso ham or andouille sausage* or hot Italian sausage, chopped
- 1 green bell pepper, chopped
- ½ small onion, chopped
- ½ carrot, chopped
- ½ leek (white and pale green parts only), chopped
- ½ celery stalk, chopped
- 1 large garlic clove, chopped
- 1²⁄₃ cups (or more) chicken stock or canned broth

Pork
- 6 tablespoons (¾ stick) butter
- 8 6-ounce pork tenderloin medallions
- 2 teaspoons Dijon mustard
- 2 teaspoons minced fresh tarragon or 1 teaspoon dried, crumbled

For bean sauce: Soak beans overnight in water to cover. Drain.

Heat oil in heavy medium saucepan over medium heat. Add ham and sauté 5 minutes. Stir in bell pepper, onion, carrot, leek, celery and garlic. Cook 10 minutes, stirring occasionally. Add 1²⁄₃ cups stock and beans. Turn heat to low. Cover and cook until beans are tender, about 1 hour 15 minutes.

Puree bean mixture in blender or food processor until smooth. Strain. (*Can be prepared 1 day ahead. Cover and chill.*)

For pork: Preheat oven to 375°F. Melt 4 tablespoons butter in heavy large ovenproof skillet over medium heat. Season pork with salt and pepper. Add to skillet and cook until golden brown on all sides, about 10 minutes. Transfer pork in skillet to oven. Roast until cooked, about 5 minutes. Let stand 10 minutes.

Heat bean sauce in heavy small saucepan over medium heat. Whisk in remaining 2 tablespoons butter, mustard and half of tarragon. Thin sauce with additional stock if desired. Season with salt and pepper. Thinly slice pork. Nap plates with sauce. Top with fanned slices of pork. Sprinkle with tarragon.

*Tasso, a spiced smoked creole ham, and *andouille, a smoked spicy pork sausage, are available at specialty foods stores and some butcher shops. Hot Italian sausage can be substituted.

Sausage Stew

6 servings

1½ pounds veal or pork sausages
¾ pound sweet Italian sausages

4 onions, sliced
2 bell peppers, chopped
6 garlic cloves, chopped
1 cup dry white wine
1 pound boiling potatoes, peeled, cubed
1 16-ounce can stewed tomatoes
1 14½-ounce can chicken broth
¼ cup tomato paste

1 10-ounce package frozen green beans
1 teaspoon dried oregano, crumbled
1 teaspoon dried basil, crumbled
1 teaspoon dried marjoram, crumbled
1 cup shredded mozzarella cheese
1 cup shredded cheddar cheese
¼ cup grated Parmesan cheese

Heat heavy 4-quart saucepan over medium-high heat. Add sausages and cook until brown, turning occasionally, about 30 minutes. Transfer sausages to plate; cool slightly. Cut into 1-inch pieces.

Remove all but 2 tablespoons fat from saucepan. Add onions to saucepan and sauté over medium heat until tender, about 15 minutes. Add bell peppers and garlic and continue cooking until bell peppers just begin to soften, about 5 minutes. Pour in wine and boil 1 minute. Add potatoes, tomatoes, broth and tomato paste. Simmer until potatoes are tender, stirring occasionally, about 10 minutes. Stir in green beans, sausages and herbs. Cover and cook 15 minutes. Add all cheeses and stir. Serve immediately.

Grilled Szechwan-Style Baby Back Ribs

These hoisin-glazed baby back ribs are irresistible.

4 servings

Marinade
1 small fresh cilantro bunch
½ fresh parsley bunch
2 garlic cloves
1 1-inch piece fresh ginger, peeled
12 cups chicken stock or canned broth
3¼ pounds baby back pork ribs (2 racks)

Sauce
⅔ cup hoisin sauce*
¼ cup plus 1 tablespoon miso (soy bean paste)*

1 tablespoon plus 1 teaspoon minced fresh ginger
1 tablespoon plus 1 teaspoon minced garlic
1 tablespoon plus 1 teaspoon sake or dry Sherry
1 tablespoon plus 1 teaspoon soy sauce
2 teaspoons sugar
2 teaspoons chili paste with garlic*

For marinade: Mince first 4 ingredients in processor or blender. Transfer to large Dutch oven. Add chicken stock and ribs. Simmer over medium heat until ribs are tender, about 30 minutes.

For sauce: Place all ingredients in medium bowl and stir to combine.

Drain ribs and transfer to baking pan. Brush with some of sauce. Let ribs cool about 1 hour. (*Can be prepared 1 day ahead. Cover ribs and remaining sauce separately; refrigerate.*)

Prepare barbecue (medium-low heat) or preheat broiler. Brush ribs with some of sauce again. Grill or broil until deep brown, about 4 minutes per side. Cut racks into individual ribs and serve with remaining sauce.

*Available at oriental markets and in the oriental section of some supermarkets.

Red Beans and Rice

Ask your butcher to cut the ham hocks for you.

8 servings

2½ cups dried red kidney beans, rinsed, picked over

½ ounce dried porcini mushrooms*
1½ cups boiling water

1½ tablespoons olive oil
1 large onion, chopped
2 celery stalks, chopped
1 large green bell pepper, chopped
2 garlic cloves, crushed
¼ cup finely chopped fresh parsley
2½ tablespoons chopped fresh tarragon or 2 teaspoons dried, crumbled
2 teaspoons minced fresh rosemary or 1 teaspoon dried, crumbled
3 bay leaves

3 ounces button mushrooms, sliced
3 14½-ounce cans beef broth
4 cups water
1¾ pounds smoked ham hocks, cut into pieces

3 tablespoons butter
1½ pounds smoked sausage (such as kielbasa or andouille)

Hot pepper sauce (such as Tabasco)
Cayenne pepper
4 cups long-grain rice, freshly cooked
¼ cup chopped fresh chives
¼ cup chopped fresh parsley

Place beans in large bowl with enough cold water to cover by 3 inches. Let beans stand overnight. Drain beans.

Place dried mushrooms in bowl and pour 1½ cups boiling water over. Soak until softened, about 15 minutes. Transfer mushrooms to bowl using slotted spoon. Strain soaking liquid through sieve lined with paper towel; reserve. Thinly slice mushrooms. Set aside.

Heat oil in heavy large pot over medium heat. Add onion, celery, bell pepper, garlic, ¼ cup parsley, tarragon, rosemary and bay leaves. Cook until vegetables are translucent, stirring occasionally, about 10 minutes. Add button mushrooms and sauté 3 minutes. Mix in kidney beans, porcini mushrooms, reserved mushroom soaking liquid, broth, 4 cups water and ham hocks. Bring to boil. Reduce heat, cover partially and simmer 1 hour.

Meanwhile, melt 3 tablespoons butter in heavy large skillet over medium heat. Add sausage and cook through, turning frequently, about 10 minutes. Transfer sausage to paper towels and drain. Cut into 1-inch-thick slices.

Add sausage to bean mixture in pot. Simmer uncovered until beans are very tender, stirring frequently, about 45 minutes. Season with hot pepper sauce and cayenne. Remove ham hocks. Discard bones. Cut meat into bite-size pieces and return to pot. (*Can be prepared 2 days ahead. Cover and refrigerate. Bring to simmer before serving.*) Spoon rice into bowls. Ladle beans over. Garnish with chopped fresh chives and parsley.

*Porcini are available at Italian markets and specialty foods stores.

🍎 Poultry and Game

Moroccan Chicken

4 to 6 servings

½ cup dried currants or raisins
¼ cup dry Sherry

3 tablespoons butter
2 tablespoons finely chopped onion
3 tablespoons all purpose flour
1½ teaspoons curry powder

1 cup milk
1 medium apple, peeled, diced

6 boneless chicken breast halves, skinned, patted dry
¼ cup slivered almonds, toasted

Place currants in small bowl. Add Sherry and let soak 2 hours.

Preheat oven to 350°F. Lightly butter 8-inch square baking pan. Melt 3 tablespoons butter in heavy medium skillet over low heat. Add onion and cook until translucent, stirring occasionally, about 4 minutes. Add flour and curry powder and stir 3 minutes. Gradually whisk in milk. Bring to boil, stirring constantly. Mix in currants with Sherry and apple. Season to taste with salt.

Arrange chicken in prepared pan in single layer. Cover with sauce. Top with almonds. Bake until chicken is cooked through, about 30 minutes.

White Chili

8 servings

1 pound dried Great Northern white beans, rinsed, picked over

2 pounds boneless chicken breasts

1 tablespoon olive oil
2 medium onions, chopped
4 garlic cloves, minced
2 4-ounce cans chopped mild green chilies
2 teaspoons ground cumin
1½ teaspoons dried oregano, crumbled

¼ teaspoon ground cloves
¼ teaspoon cayenne pepper
6 cups chicken stock or canned broth

3 cups grated Monterey Jack cheese (about 12 ounces)
Sour cream
Salsa
Chopped fresh cilantro

Place beans in heavy large pot. Add enough cold water to cover by at least 3 inches and soak overnight.

Place chicken in heavy large saucepan. Add cold water to cover and bring to simmer. Cook until just tender, about 15 minutes. Drain and cool. Remove skin. Cut chicken into cubes. Set aside.

Drain beans. Heat oil in same pot over medium-high heat. Add onions and sauté until translucent, about 10 minutes. Stir in garlic, then chilies, cumin, oregano, cloves and cayenne and sauté 2 minutes. Add beans and stock and bring to boil. Reduce heat and simmer until beans are very tender, stirring occasionally, about 2 hours. (*Can be prepared 1 day ahead. Cover and refrigerate. Bring to simmer before continuing.*)

Add chicken and 1 cup cheese to chili and stir until cheese melts. Season to taste with salt and pepper. Ladle chili into bowls. Serve with remaining cheese, sour cream, salsa and chopped cilantro.

Sautéed Quail with Rice and Pecans

8 servings

¼ cup plus 5 tablespoons olive oil
½ cup minced yellow onion
2 cups long-grain rice
4 cups chicken stock or canned broth

2 tablespoons cider vinegar
4 green onions, thinly sliced

⅓ cup dried currants
⅔ cup toasted pecans

8 quail

Red and/or green grape clusters

Heat 2 tablespoons olive oil in heavy medium saucepan over medium heat. Add minced onion and sauté until translucent, about 6 minutes. Add 2 cups rice and stir until grains are opaque, 30 seconds. Add 4 cups chicken stock and bring to simmer, stirring occasionally. Reduce heat to low. Cover and cook until rice is tender and stock is absorbed, 20 minutes. Transfer to large bowl and cool.

Whisk ¼ cup olive oil and 2 tablespoons cider vinegar in small bowl. Mix in sliced green onions, dried currants and toasted pecans. Add to rice and toss to combine. Season generously with salt and pepper. (*Rice mixture can be prepared 6 hours ahead. Cover tightly and let stand at room temperature.*)

Arrange 1 quail breast side down on work surface. Cut along each side of backbone and remove backbone. Press quail open. Using small sharp knife, carefully cut between rib bones and meat; remove ribs. Cut along each side of breastbone (do not cut through skin) and remove. Cut out wishbone. Repeat with remaining quail. Brush quail with remaining 3 tablespoons olive oil. Season generously with salt and pepper. Heat heavy large nonstick skillet over high heat. Add quail and cook until brown on all sides and cooked through, turning occasionally, about 6 minutes.

Arrange rice on large platter. Surround with quail. Garnish platter with grapes and serve immediately.

Turkey Cutlets with Paprika Cream Sauce

2 servings

2 tablespoons (¼ stick) butter
½ onion, chopped
1 teaspoon paprika
½ cup whipping cream
1 teaspoon Dijon mustard
2 teaspoons minced fresh dill

¾ pound turkey breast cutlets
All purpose flour

Melt 1 tablespoon butter in heavy medium skillet over medium heat. Add onion and sauté until tender, about 8 minutes. Add paprika and stir 1 minute. Add cream. Simmer until slightly thickened, about 1 minute. Mix in mustard and dill. Season sauce with salt and pepper. Cover and set aside.

Season turkey with salt and pepper. Dredge in flour. Melt remaining 1 tablespoon butter in heavy large skillet over medium-high heat. Add turkey and sauté until just cooked through, about 1 minute per side. Transfer to plates. Spoon sauce over and serve.

Roast Chicken with Olives and Potatoes

A superb dish—and what could be simpler? Large roasting chickens can be ordered from the supermarket or butcher if you call a day or two ahead. Serve steamed green beans and French bread on the side.

4 servings

1 7-pound roasting chicken
6 tablespoons olive paste (olivada)*
2 bay leaves
  Olive oil
4 tablespoons fresh thyme leaves

4 medium russet potatoes, peeled, cut into 1½-inch pieces
2 tablespoons olive oil
½ cup Kalamata** olives

Fresh thyme leaves

Preheat oven to 450°F. Slide hand between chicken skin and meat over breast and legs to form pockets. Spread 4 tablespoons olive paste over breast and leg meat of chicken. Spread remaining 2 tablespoons olive paste in cavity of chicken. Place bay leaves in cavity. Tie legs together to hold shape. Rub olive oil into chicken skin. Sprinkle with salt and pepper. Sprinkle with 2 tablespoons thyme. Place chicken in large roasting pan.

Place potatoes in large bowl. Add 2 tablespoons olive oil and salt and pepper to taste and toss to coat. Sprinkle with 2 tablespoons thyme. Add potatoes to pan with chicken. Roast 15 minutes. Reduce oven temperature to 375°F and roast 1 hour longer. Add olives to pan. Continue roasting until juices run clear when chicken is pierced in thickest part of thigh, basting occasionally with pan juices, about 10 minutes.

Transfer chicken to platter. Surround with potatoes and olives. Sprinkle with additional thyme. Pour chicken pan juices into large cup and degrease. Serve chicken, passing pan juices separately.

*Olive paste, also called *olivada,* is available at Italian markets and specialty foods stores. If unavailable, puree ½ cup pitted black, brine-cured olives (such as Kalamata) in processor.
**Kalamata olives are available at Greek and Italian markets and at some specialty foods stores.

Roast Cornish Game Hens in Herbed Breadcrumb Crust

2 servings

2 white-bread slices, crusts trimmed
1 cup chopped fresh parsley
1 tablespoon grated Parmesan cheese
1 shallot, chopped
1 garlic clove, chopped

2 Cornish game hens
3 tablespoons extra-virgin olive oil
4 teaspoons Dijon mustard

Blend bread, parsley, Parmesan, shallot and garlic in processor until crumbs form. Season with salt and pepper. Set crumbs aside.

Preheat oven to 350°F. Cut game hens along spines. Open hens and arrange skin side up on work surface. Pound with side of cleaver or heavy large knife to flatten slightly. Season with salt and pepper. Drizzle 1 tablespoon oil over hens. Spread mustard on skin sides. Sprinkle with crumbs, pressing to adhere. Heat remaining 2 tablespoons oil in heavy large ovenproof skillet over medium heat. Add hens crumb side down and cook 5 minutes. Turn and cook 5 minutes. Transfer pan with hens to oven and roast until hens are golden brown and just tender, about 35 minutes. Serve.

Island Chicken with Ginger-Lime Sauce

If time is running short, the chicken is just as delicious without the noodles.

6 servings

Marinade
- 1 small fresh cilantro bunch
- 2 garlic cloves
- 1 12-inch lemongrass stalk,* cut into ½-inch pieces
- 1 shallot or 2 green onions, quartered
- ¾ cup canned coconut milk*
- ¼ cup peanut oil
- 2 teaspoons fresh lemon juice
- ½ teaspoon pepper
- 6 boneless chicken breast halves

Sauce
- 3 cups chicken stock or canned low-salt broth
- 2 tablespoons minced fresh ginger

Stir-Fry
- 1 cup fresh shiitake mushrooms (about 4 ounces)**
- ¾ cup snow peas
- ½ red or yellow bell pepper
- 2 celery stalks
- 1 large carrot
- 1 tomato, peeled, seeded
- 4 tablespoons olive oil
- 1 tablespoon oriental sesame oil
- ¾ cup bean sprouts
- 2 teaspoons minced fresh ginger
- 1 garlic clove, minced
- 1 small bunch fresh cilantro, chopped
- 1 tablespoon soy sauce
- 4 tablespoons (½ stick) unsalted butter
- 2 tablespoons fresh lime juice

Crispy Noodle Pancakes (see recipe)

For marinade: Mince fresh cilantro, garlic cloves, lemongrass stalk and shallot in processor or blender. Transfer to large bowl. Stir in coconut milk, oil, lemon juice and pepper. Season with salt. Add chicken and marinate 1 hour.

For sauce: Remove chicken from marinade. Place marinade, chicken stock and minced fresh ginger in heavy large saucepan. Boil until sauce is reduced to 1 cup, skimming any fat from surface, about 25 minutes. Strain. (*Sauce can be prepared 1 day ahead. Cover chicken and sauce separately; refrigerate.*)

For stir-fry: Cut mushrooms, snow peas, bell pepper, celery, carrot and tomato into matchstick-size strips. Heat 2 tablespoons olive oil in heavy large skillet over medium heat. Pat chicken dry. Add to skillet and sauté until cooked through, about 4 minutes per side. Transfer to plate. Tent with foil.

Heat remaining 2 tablespoons olive oil and 1 tablespoon sesame oil in wok or heavy large skillet over high heat. Add mushrooms, snow peas, bell pepper, celery, carrot and bean sprouts to skillet. Stir-fry 1 minute. Mix in minced fresh ginger and garlic. Cook 30 seconds. Stir in tomato and chopped fresh cilantro. Cook 1 minute. Add soy sauce.

Bring sauce to simmer in heavy small saucepan over medium heat. Whisk in butter and fresh lime juice.

Place 1 Crispy Noodle Pancake on each plate. Top with stir-fried vegetables. Cut chicken into thin slices and fan atop stir-fried vegetables. Pour sauce around chicken and serve immediately.

*Available at Indian, Southeast Asian or Latin American markets.

**If unavailable, ½ ounce dried *shiitake* mushrooms can be substituted. Soak in hot water to cover until softened, about 30 minutes. Drain. Squeeze out excess moisture and discard hard stems.

Crispy Noodle Pancakes

Makes 6

6 ounces fresh chow mein noodles
4 tablespoons olive oil

4½ teaspoons oriental sesame oil

Add chow mein noodles to large pot of boiling water. Return to boil and cook 1½ minutes, stirring occasionally. Drain. Rinse noodles with cold water. Drain well. Mix with 1 tablespoon olive oil.

Divide noodles into 6 portions. Heat 1 tablespoon olive oil and 1½ teaspoons sesame oil in heavy large skillet over medium heat. Add 2 noodle portions. Flatten slightly to 6-inch rounds. Cook until golden brown, about 6 minutes per side. Transfer to paper towels. Repeat with remaining oil and noodles in 2 more batches. (*Noodle pancakes can be prepared up to 15 minutes ahead. Keep warm in 200°F oven.*)

Duck, Lamb and Sausage Cassoulet

A new version of a French classic—hearty and sophisticated. It can be assembled one day ahead and then reheated before serving.

10 servings

1½ pounds Great Northern white beans, rinsed, picked over

10 cups (about) chicken stock or canned broth
4 cups water
2 large carrots, chopped
5 large white onions, chopped
2 pounds smoked kielbasa sausage
½ pound thick-sliced smoked bacon, diced
14 large garlic cloves, minced
6 fresh parsley sprigs

3 bay leaves
6 teaspoons dried thyme, crumbled

2 5-pound ducks

2 pounds boned lamb leg, fat trimmed, cut into 1½-inch pieces
4 28-ounce cans Italian plum tomatoes, drained (juices reserved), chopped
2 cups dry white wine

1 cup chopped fresh parsley

Place white beans in large saucepan. Add enough cold water to cover by 3 inches and let beans soak overnight.

Drain beans. Return beans to saucepan. Add 8 cups stock, 4 cups water, carrots and half of chopped onions. Bring to boil. Reduce heat and simmer 30 minutes. Add sausage, bacon, ⅓ of garlic, parsley sprigs, 2 bay leaves and 1 teaspoon thyme. Simmer until beans are just tender, stirring occasionally, about 20 minutes longer. Discard bay leaves and parsley. Remove sausage. Cool slightly. Cut sausage into ½-inch-thick rounds. Transfer sausage to large bowl; cover and refrigerate. Drain beans; reserve cooking liquid.

Preheat oven to 325°F. Place ducks on rack on roasting pan. Pierce skin (not meat) with fork. Roast until ducks are cooked through and legs move easily, pouring off fat in pan and reserving ⅓ cup fat, about 2 hours. Cool ducks completely. Cut off duck legs and wings and reserve. Discard duck skin and fat from breasts and thighs. Cut breast and thigh meat into ½- to ¾-inch pieces. Add cut-up duck meat to sausage in bowl. Cover meat mixture and duck legs and wings separately; refrigerate until ready to use.

Heat ⅓ cup reserved duck fat in heavy large skillet over high heat. Add half of lamb and brown well. Using slotted spoon, remove lamb and add to meat mixture. Repeat with remaining lamb. Season meat mixture with salt and pepper. Reduce heat to medium-low. Add remaining onions and garlic to skillet and cook until onions are tender, stirring occasionally, about 8 minutes. Add 1 cup

bean cooking liquid and bring to boil, scraping up any browned bits. Transfer mixture to heavy large saucepan. Add remaining bean cooking liquid, tomatoes, wine, 2 teaspoons thyme and 1 bay leaf. Cook sauce over medium heat until reduced to 7 cups, stirring occasionally.

Spread ⅓ of beans in bottom of 10-quart Dutch oven or divide between two 5-quart Dutch ovens. Season generously with salt and pepper. Top with half of meat mixture. Sprinkle with ¼ cup parsley and 1½ teaspoons thyme. Top with 2⅓ cups sauce. Spread ⅓ of beans over. Season generously with salt and pepper. Top with remaining meat mixture. Sprinkle ½ cup parsley and remaining 1½ teaspoons thyme over. Top with 2⅓ cups sauce. Spread remaining beans over. Season generously with salt and pepper. Pour remaining 2⅓ cups sauce over. Top with reserved duck legs and wings. (*Can be prepared 1 day ahead. Cover and refrigerate. Bring to room temperature before baking.*)

Preheat oven to 350°F. Cover cassoulet and bake until heated through, adding enough reserved tomato juices and/or remaining stock as necessary if mixture seems dry, about 2 hours. Sprinkle with remaining ¼ cup parsley.

❦ *Fish and Shellfish*

Tuna with Spinach and Coconut Sauce

2 servings

1¼ cups bottled clam juice
5 tablespoons unsalted butter
3 green onions (green part only), finely chopped
1 small carrot, peeled, cut into matchstick-size strips
1 celery stalk, cut into matchstick-size strips

1 teaspoon minced peeled fresh ginger
1 teaspoon minced garlic
¼ cup unsweetened coconut milk*
¼ cup whipping cream

1 small bunch fresh spinach, stems trimmed
2 6-ounce 1-inch-thick tuna steaks

Boil clam juice in heavy small skillet until reduced to ⅓ cup, about 10 minutes. Melt 2 tablespoons butter in heavy large skillet over medium heat. Add green onions, carrot, celery, ginger and minced garlic and sauté 1 minute. Reduce heat to medium. Add reduced clam juice, coconut milk and cream. Season to taste with salt and pepper. Cook until vegetables are crisp-tender and sauce thickens, stirring occasionally, about 5 minutes.

Meanwhile, melt 1 tablespoon butter in heavy large skillet over medium heat. Add spinach and stir until wilted. Divide spinach between plates. Tent with foil to keep warm. Melt remaining 2 tablespoons butter in same skillet over medium-high heat. Add tuna steaks to skillet and cook to desired doneness, about 3 minutes per side for medium.

Place tuna steaks atop spinach. Spoon sauce over fish and serve.

*Available canned at Indian, Southeast Asian and Latin American markets.

Manhattan-Style Seafood Stew

Tropical Chicken Salad

Spinach Linguine with Goat Cheese

Ann Mitchell

Warm Lamb Salad with Mixed Greens

Bret Lopez

*Turkey Cutlets with Paprika Cream Sauce
and Noodles with Poppy Seeds and Peas*

Cheese Ravioli with Old-fashioned Meat Sauce

Roast Chicken with Olives and Potatoes

Roast Leg of Lamb with Pesto,
Radicchio and Shallots

David Bishop

Sautéed Scallops with Shiitake Mushrooms and Broccoli

2 servings

1 ounce dried shiitake mushrooms
1 pound broccoli, trimmed, cut into florets
¼ cup butter
¾ pound sea scallops, halved crosswise

1 bunch green onions, sliced
½ lemon
2 tablespoons toasted pine nuts
Freshly cooked rice

Place mushrooms in small bowl. Add boiling water to cover. Let stand until softened, about 20 minutes. Drain, reserving 3 tablespoons soaking liquid. Squeeze out any liquid from mushrooms. Cut out stems; cut mushrooms into quarters. Blanch broccoli in large pot of boiling salted water until just crisp-tender. Drain. Refresh with cold water and drain well.

Melt butter in heavy large skillet over medium-high heat. Add mushrooms and sauté 1 minute. Add scallops and green onions and stir until scallops are almost cooked through. Add broccoli and stir until broccoli is heated through and scallops are opaque. Add reserved shiitake soaking liquid. Squeeze juice of lemon half into skillet. Season mixture with salt and pepper. Sprinkle with nuts. Serve scallops immediately with rice.

Manhattan-Style Seafood Stew

4 servings

5 bacon slices, chopped
1½ large onions, chopped
5 large shallots or green onions, chopped
3 28-ounce cans Italian plum tomatoes, drained
3 8-ounce bottles clam juice
¾ cup dry white wine
3 bay leaves
¼ teaspoon (generous) dried crushed red pepper

1 pound White Rose potatoes, peeled, quartered lengthwise, thinly sliced
24 clams (about 3½ pounds), well scrubbed
½ pound sea scallops, halved crosswise
½ pound uncooked medium shrimp, peeled, deveined (tails left intact)
30 fresh basil leaves, thinly sliced
1 tablespoon matchstick-size strips of lemon peel

Cook bacon in heavy large pot over medium heat until fat renders, about 5 minutes. Add onions and shallots and sauté until tender, about 8 minutes. Chop tomatoes in processor. Add to pot with clam juice, wine, bay leaves and dried red pepper. Simmer 20 minutes, stirring occasionally.

Add potatoes to stew and simmer until tender, about 20 minutes. Season with salt and pepper. (*Can be prepared 1 day ahead. Cover and refrigerate. Return to simmer before continuing.*) Add clams to stew. Cover and simmer until clams begin to open, about 5 minutes. Add scallops and shrimp. Cover and simmer until clams open and scallops and shrimp are cooked through, about 3 minutes. Discard any clams that do not open. Mix in half of basil. Transfer stew to large serving bowl. Sprinkle with remaining basil and lemon peel.

Grilled Pompano with Spinach and Cherry Tomatoes

8 servings

8 whole pompano, cleaned, scaled, or 8 6-ounce tilapia or butterfish fillets
Olive oil

3 tablespoons olive oil
2 shallots or green onions, minced
4 large spinach bunches, stemmed
2 1-pint baskets red or yellow cherry tomatoes

Prepare barbecue (high heat). Brush fish with oil. Season with salt and pepper. Grill fish until just cooked through, about 3 minutes per side for whole fish and 2 minutes per side for fillets.

Meanwhile, heat 2 tablespoons oil in heavy large deep skillet over high heat. Add shallots and sauté 2 minutes. Add spinach and sauté until wilted, about 3 minutes. Season to taste with salt and pepper. Transfer spinach to platter. Tent with foil to keep warm. Heat remaining 1 tablespoon oil in same skillet over high heat. Add tomatoes and sauté until heated through, about 2 minutes. Season to taste with salt and pepper.

Arrange fish atop spinach on platter. Surround with tomatoes and serve.

Creamy Smoked Salmon and Dill Tart

Purchased phyllo pastry is used here instead of a regular pie crust for quick and easy assembly. This tart is best when served at room temperature.

6 servings

5 frozen phyllo pastry sheets, thawed
3 tablespoons unsalted butter, melted

4 large egg yolks
1 tablespoon plus 1 teaspoon Dijon mustard
3 large eggs

1 cup half and half
1 cup whipping cream
6 ounces smoked salmon, chopped
4 green onions, chopped
¼ cup chopped fresh dill or 1 tablespoon dried dillweed
Dill sprigs

Generously butter 9½-inch-diameter deep-dish pie plate. Place 1 phyllo sheet on work surface (cover remaining pieces with plastic wrap, then with clean damp towel). Brush phyllo sheet with butter and fold in half lengthwise. Brush folded surface with butter. Cut in half crosswise. Place 1 phyllo rectangle, buttered side down, in prepared pie plate, covering bottom and letting pastry overhang 1 section of edge by ½ inch. Brush top of phyllo in pie plate with butter. Place second phyllo rectangle in pie plate, covering bottom and letting pastry overhang another section of edge by ½ inch; brush with butter. Repeat process with remaining 4 phyllo sheets, making certain entire surface of edge is covered to form crust. Fold overhang under to form crust edge flush with edge of pie plate. Brush crust edges with butter. (*Can be prepared 4 hours ahead. Refrigerate.*)

Preheat oven to 350°F. Whisk yolks and mustard in medium bowl to blend. Beat in eggs, half and half, cream, salmon, onions and chopped dill. Season to taste with salt and pepper. Pour into prepared crust. Bake until center is set, about 50 minutes. Transfer to rack. Cool. Garnish with dill sprigs and serve slightly warm or at room temperature.

Crispy Fish with Sweet-and-Sour Sauce

4 servings

1 pound sea bass fillets, cut into ³/₄-inch-wide slices
3 tablespoons cornstarch
1 cup all purpose flour
4 tablespoons vegetable oil
2 teaspoons baking powder
½ teaspoon salt
1 cup water

1 cup pineapple juice
6 tablespoons sugar
¼ cup red wine vinegar

¼ teaspoon hot pepper sauce (such as Tabasco)
⅛ teaspoon salt
1 teaspoon grated peeled fresh ginger
1 teaspoon grated lemon peel
1 red bell pepper, cut into matchstick-size strips

4 cups vegetable oil (for deep frying)

Toss fish pieces with 2 tablespoons cornstarch in medium bowl to coat. Mix flour, 3 tablespoons oil, baking powder and ½ teaspoon salt in small bowl. Gradually add water, whisking until batter is smooth. Pour batter over fish and stir to coat. Let stand 15 minutes.

Whisk remaining 1 tablespoon cornstarch, pineapple juice, sugar, vinegar, hot pepper sauce and ⅛ teaspoon salt in small bowl to blend. Heat remaining 1 tablespoon oil in heavy medium skillet over medium-high heat. Add ginger and lemon peel and stir-fry until fragrant, about 30 seconds. Add bell pepper and stir-fry just to heat through, about 30 seconds. Add pineapple juice mixture and cook until sauce is thick and clear, stirring constantly, about 1 minute.

Heat 4 cups oil in wok or deep medium saucepan to 375°F. Add batter-coated fish pieces to oil in batches and fry until crisp and golden, about 4 minutes. Using slotted spoon, transfer fish to paper towel-lined dish and drain. Reheat oil if necessary between batches.

Arrange fish on platter. Reheat sauce briefly, spoon over fish and serve.

Shrimp with Almond Rice Pilaf

2 servings

1 cup canned chicken broth
1 cup instant rice
1 cup frozen peas, thawed
1 2-ounce package slivered almonds, toasted

¼ cup (½ stick) butter
4 garlic cloves, minced
1 tablespoon lemon juice
1 teaspoon paprika
½ pound medium shrimp, peeled, deveined

Bring chicken broth to boil in heavy medium saucepan. Mix in rice. Cover and remove from heat. Let stand until liquid is absorbed, approximately 5 minutes. Stir in peas and toasted slivered almonds.

Melt butter in heavy medium skillet over medium-high heat. Add garlic, lemon juice and paprika and cook until garlic is golden, stirring occasionally, about 2 minutes. Add shrimp and cook until opaque, stirring constantly, about 4 minutes. Stir in rice mixture and cook until heated through, stirring constantly, about 2 more minutes. Serve hot.

Pecan- and Bran-crusted Catfish

6 servings

2 shallots or 4 green onions, minced
2 garlic cloves, minced
2 tablespoons purchased teriyaki
 marinade and sauce
2 tablespoons chopped fresh basil
 or 1 teaspoon dried, crumbled
1 tablespoon chopped fresh cilantro
1 teaspoon minced fresh ginger
6 6-ounce catfish fillets

3¼ cups bran flakes
1 cup pecans (about 3½ ounces)

1 cup fresh egg-bread breadcrumbs
1 tablespoon ground pepper
 All purpose flour
3 eggs, beaten to blend

6 tablespoons (¾ stick) butter
6 tablespoons olive oil
1 shallot or 2 green onions, minced
2 tablespoons chopped fresh basil
1 tablespoon chopped fresh
 cilantro

Combine first 6 ingredients in small bowl. Place fish in glass baking dish. Spoon marinade mixture over both sides of fish. Cover and refrigerate 2 hours.

Finely grind bran flakes in processor. Add pecans and process until finely ground. Transfer to large bowl. Mix in breadcrumbs and pepper. Season with salt. Place flour in second large bowl. Pour eggs into third large bowl. Remove fish from marinade. Coat fish with flour; shake off excess. Dip fish into eggs and then coat with breadcrumb mixture, pressing to adhere.

Melt butter with oil in heavy large skillet over medium heat. Add fish in batches and cook until golden brown and cooked through, about 5 minutes per side. Sprinkle 1 shallot, 2 tablespoons basil and 1 tablespoon cilantro over fish.

Red Snapper Roasted with Fennel and Breadcrumbs

If one large fish is difficult to find, two smaller ones can be substituted.

6 servings

2 fresh fennel bulbs, trimmed,
 chopped
6 large shallots or green onions,
 chopped
½ cup chopped fresh Italian parsley
2 cups fresh French-bread
 breadcrumbs
¼ cup olive oil

1 3½- to 4-pound headless red
 snapper
¼ cup dry white wine
 Olive oil

Combine first 3 ingredients in medium bowl. Transfer 1 cup fennel mixture to large bowl. Add breadcrumbs and ¼ cup olive oil to 1 cup fennel mixture in large bowl. Season with salt and pepper. (*Can be prepared 1 day ahead. Cover fennel mixture and breadcrumb mixture separately and refrigerate.*)

Preheat oven to 450°F. Cut slashes 2 inches apart almost to bone in both sides of fish. Spread half of fennel mixture in bottom of gratin dish or roasting pan. Sprinkle with wine. Spread generous amount of oil over inside and outside of fish. Season inside and out with salt and pepper. Set fish atop fennel mixture in dish. Spread remaining fennel mixture inside fish. Spread breadcrumb mixture over top of fish, pressing to adhere.

Bake fish until just opaque in center, about 45 minutes. Serve with fennel.

Shrimp and Mushrooms in Spicy Black Bean Oyster Sauce

4 servings

12 medium-size dried Chinese black mushrooms* or dried shiitake mushrooms (about 1 ounce)
1½ cups hot water
1 pound large uncooked shrimp, peeled, deveined
1 tablespoon dry Sherry or dry white wine
2 tablespoons cornstarch

2 tablespoons oyster sauce*
1½ teaspoons sugar

2 tablespoons salted black beans*
1½ tablespoons minced garlic
1½ tablespoons minced peeled fresh ginger
1 tablespoon minced seeded red or green chili (such as serrano or jalapeño)
2 green onions, finely chopped

¼ cup plus 2 tablespoons peanut oil

Freshly cooked rice

Soak mushrooms in 1½ cups hot water in medium bowl until softened, about 20 minutes. Drain mushrooms, reserving 1 cup soaking liquid. Squeeze out excess moisture. Cut off stems and discard. Cut caps in half. Toss mushrooms, shrimp, Sherry and 1 tablespoon cornstarch together in medium bowl to coat evenly. Let stand 15 minutes.

Whisk 1 cup reserved mushroom soaking liquid, oyster sauce, remaining 1 tablespoon cornstarch and sugar in small bowl until cornstarch dissolves. Cover beans with hot water and soak 1 minute. Drain beans and chop finely. Combine beans in bowl with garlic, ginger, chili and half of green onions.

Heat ¼ cup oil in wok or heavy large skillet over high heat. Add shrimp mixture and stir-fry until shrimp curl and turn pink, about 2 minutes. Pour contents of wok into sieve to drain shrimp.

Line platter with cooked rice. Heat remaining 2 tablespoons peanut oil in same wok over high heat. Stir-fry black bean mixture until fragrant, about 1 minute. Return shrimp mixture to wok. Stir mushroom liquid mixture and add to wok. Cook until sauce thickens and begins to boil, stirring constantly, about 1 minute. Spoon contents of wok over rice on platter. Garnish with remaining green onions and serve immediately.

*Available at oriental markets and some supermarkets.

Baked Fish with Tomatoes and Garlic

2 servings

2 tablespoons olive oil
2 6-ounce sole fillets
1 large tomato, seeded, chopped

1 tablespoon minced garlic
1 tablespoon chopped fresh parsley

Preheat oven to 400°F. Brush small, shallow ovenproof baking dish with small amount of olive oil. Place fillets in dish and season with salt and pepper. Combine remaining olive oil with tomato and garlic in small bowl. Spoon over fillets. Bake until fillets are just cooked through, about 15 minutes. Sprinkle with chopped parsley and serve immediately.

Shark Steak au Poivre

Fish gets a traditional beef treatment with absolutely delicious results.

6 servings

3 tablespoons butter
3 tablespoons chopped shallots
⅓ cup Cognac or other brandy
1 cup chicken stock or canned low-salt broth
½ cup beef stock or canned unsalted broth

2 cups whipping cream
6 1½-inch-thick shark steaks (about 6 ounces each)
2 tablespoons coarsely ground pepper

Melt 1 tablespoon butter in heavy medium saucepan over medium-high heat. Add shallots and sauté until just tender, about 3 minutes. Add Cognac and simmer until liquid is reduced to 1 tablespoon, about 4 minutes. Stir in chicken and beef stock. Simmer until reduced to ⅓ cup, about 10 minutes. (*Can be prepared 1 day ahead. Cover and refrigerate.*)

Bring stock mixture to boil. Add cream and simmer until liquid is reduced to 1½ cups, about 20 minutes. Season with salt. Keep warm.

Pat shark steaks dry. Season with salt. Sprinkle both sides of shark generously with pepper. Melt remaining 2 tablespoons butter in heavy large skillet over medium-high heat. Add shark and fry until cooked through, about 4 minutes per side. Transfer to plates. Spoon sauce over and serve.

🍎 *Eggs, Cheese and Vegetables*

Banana Bread French Toast

6 servings

Banana Bread
2 cups sifted all purpose flour
1 teaspoon baking soda
½ teaspoon salt
½ cup (1 stick) unsalted butter, room temperature
1 cup sugar
2 eggs
1 cup mashed ripe bananas (about 2 bananas)
1 teaspoon fresh lemon juice
⅓ cup milk
½ cup chopped pecans

French Toast
4 large eggs
¼ cup whipping cream
2 tablespoons brown sugar
1 teaspoon vanilla extract
¼ teaspoon ground nutmeg
¼ teaspoon ground cinnamon

3 tablespoons (about) butter
Maple syrup

For bread: Preheat oven to 350°F. Generously butter 9 × 5 × 3-inch loaf pan. Sift first 3 ingredients into small bowl. Using electric mixer, cream butter in large bowl until light. Gradually beat in sugar. Beat in eggs 1 at a time. Add mashed bananas and lemon juice and beat until well blended. Mix in dry ingredients alternately with milk, beginning and ending with dry ingredients. Mix in pecans. Pour batter into prepared pan. Bake until tester inserted in center comes out clean, about 1 hour 20 minutes. Cool in pan on rack 10 minutes. Turn out onto rack and cool. (*Can be prepared 2 days ahead. Wrap tightly and refrigerate.*) Cut bread into ¾-inch-thick slices.

For French toast: Preheat oven to low. Whisk eggs, cream, sugar, vanilla and spices in large bowl until blended.

Melt 1 tablespoon butter in heavy large skillet over medium heat. Place some bread in batter and turn to coat thoroughly. Add bread to skillet. Cook until golden brown, about 3 minutes per side. Transfer French toast to cookie sheet; place in oven to keep warm. Repeat with remaining bread slices and batter in batches, adding more butter to skillet as necessary. Serve French toast, passing maple syrup separately.

Spinach Puff Pastry Quiche

6 servings

½ 17¼-ounce package (1 sheet) frozen puff pastry, thawed
1 3-ounce package cream cheese, room temperature
⅓ cup half and half
3 eggs
1 10-ounce package frozen chopped spinach, thawed, drained

½ cup grated cheddar cheese
¼ cup grated Parmesan cheese
2 green onions, sliced
¼ teaspoon salt
¼ teaspoon pepper

Preheat oven to 425°F. Roll puff pastry to 11-inch square. Transfer to 9-inch-diameter glass pie plate. Trim edges. Beat cream cheese in medium bowl until smooth. Gradually beat in half and half and eggs. Mix in remaining ingredients. Pour mixture into prepared crust. Bake until crust is golden brown and filling is set, about 25 minutes. Cool 10 minutes before serving.

Blackberry Oatmeal Pancakes

Makes about 8

2 cups rolled oats
2 cups buttermilk

2 eggs, beaten to blend
¼ cup (½ stick) butter, melted
½ cup all purpose flour
1 tablespoon sugar
1 teaspoon baking powder
1 teaspoon baking soda

¼ teaspoon ground cinnamon
Pinch of ground nutmeg
Pinch of salt
Vegetable oil
2 cups fresh blackberries or frozen blackberries, thawed, drained
Warm maple syrup

Mix oats and buttermilk in large bowl. Cover and refrigerate overnight.

Whisk eggs and butter into oatmeal mixture. Mix in flour, sugar, baking powder, baking soda, cinnamon, nutmeg and salt. Heat griddle or heavy large skillet over medium-high heat. Lightly brush with oil. Ladle batter by ½ cupfuls onto griddle. Sprinkle some berries over. Cook until batter bubbles and bottom is deep golden brown, about 3 minutes. Turn pancakes and cook until second sides are deep golden brown, about 3 more minutes. Transfer to plates. Repeat with remaining batter and berries. Serve with warm maple syrup.

Vegetable Lasagne with Tomato Sauce

8 servings

Carrot Layer
1 16-ounce bag frozen carrots
2 tablespoons (¼ stick) unsalted butter
¼ cup minced onion
1 7½-ounce container ricotta cheese

Spinach Layer
2 10-ounce packages frozen spinach
1 tablespoon olive oil
2 shallots or green onions, chopped
1 7½-ounce container ricotta cheese
1 egg

Eggplant Layer
1 medium eggplant, cut into ⅜-inch-thick slices
6 tablespoons olive oil
3 garlic cloves, minced

1 pound lasagne noodles

2½ cups Tomato Sauce (see recipe)
4 tablespoons chopped fresh basil
4 cups grated mozzarella cheese (about 1 pound)
3 cups grated Parmesan cheese (about 12 ounces)

For carrot layer: Cook frozen carrots in large saucepan of boiling water until soft, about 15 minutes. Drain. Melt butter in heavy large skillet over medium-high heat. Add onion and sauté 3 minutes. Puree carrots with onion and ricotta in processor. Add salt and pepper. (*Can be prepared 1 day ahead. Chill.*)

For spinach layer: Cook spinach according to package instructions. Drain and cool. Squeeze out excess water. Transfer to processor. Heat oil in heavy small skillet over medium-high heat. Add shallots and sauté 2 minutes. Add to processor. Add ricotta and egg to processor and puree mixture. Season with salt and pepper. (*Can be prepared 1 day ahead. Cover and refrigerate.*)

For eggplant layer: Salt eggplant and place between paper towels. Let stand 30 minutes. Heat 2 tablespoons oil and 1 minced garlic clove in heavy large skillet over medium heat. Add eggplant in single layer and cook until tender and golden, turning occasionally, about 10 minutes. Transfer to paper towels to drain. Repeat with remaining oil, minced garlic and eggplant in 2 more batches. Season eggplant with pepper.

Cook noodles in large pot of boiling salted water until just tender but still firm to bite, stirring occasionally. Drain. Rinse under cold water to cool; drain.

Butter 9 × 13 × 2-inch baking dish. Spread ½ cup tomato sauce on bottom of dish. Arrange ¼ of noodles over. Season with salt and pepper. Spread carrot puree over. Spoon ½ cup tomato sauce over. Sprinkle with 1 tablespoon basil, 1 cup mozzarella and ¾ cup Parmesan cheese. Top with ¼ of noodles. Season with salt and pepper. Spread spinach mixture over. Spread ½ cup tomato sauce over. Sprinkle with 1 tablespoon basil, 1 cup mozzarella and ¾ cup Parmesan cheese. Top with ¼ of noodles. Season with salt and pepper. Arrange eggplant in overlapping slices atop noodles. Spread with ½ cup tomato sauce. Sprinkle with 1 tablespoon basil, 1 cup mozzarella and ¾ cup Parmesan cheese. Top with remaining ¼ of noodles. Season with salt and pepper. Spread ½ cup tomato sauce over. Sprinkle with remaining 1 tablespoon basil, 1 cup mozzarella and ¾ cup Parmesan cheese. (*Can be prepared 1 day ahead. Cover and refrigerate. Let stand 2 hours at room temperature before continuing.*)

Preheat oven to 350°F. Bake lasagne until heated through, about 1 hour 15 minutes. Cool 10 minutes before serving.

Tomato Sauce

Makes 4 cups

1 tablespoon olive oil
1 medium onion, chopped
3 garlic cloves, minced
1 28-ounce can tomato puree
1 14- to 16-ounce can whole tomatoes, drained
1 14-ounce can crushed tomatoes
¼ cup tomato paste
¼ cup chopped fresh basil
2 tablespoons whiskey (optional)
1 tablespoon fresh lemon juice
1 teaspoon pepper
1 teaspoon grated lemon peel
⅛ teaspoon cayenne
⅛ teaspoon salt
Pinch of sugar

Heat oil in heavy large saucepan over medium heat. Add onion and garlic and sauté until onion is translucent, about 5 minutes. Add all remaining ingredients and bring to boil. Reduce heat and simmer until reduced to 4 cups, breaking up whole tomatoes with spoon and stirring occasionally, about 45 minutes. (*Tomato Sauce can be prepared 3 days ahead. Cover and refrigerate.*)

Polenta Gratin with Salsa Roja

Hearty and spicy. Great with a tossed salad for lunch or for a casual dinner.

6 servings

Salsa Roja
1 tablespoon olive oil
¾ cup chopped onion
4 garlic cloves, chopped
½ teaspoon ground cumin
1 16-ounce can tomatoes, chopped (juices reserved)
2 teaspoons minced canned chipotle chilies in adobo sauce*

Polenta
Olive oil
4½ cups water
½ teaspoon salt
Pinch of cayenne pepper
1 cup yellow cornmeal
⅔ cup lightly packed shredded cheddar cheese (about 3 ounces)

Vegetables
1 tablespoon olive oil
3½ cups sliced mushrooms
2 garlic cloves, minced
¼ teaspoon ground cumin
1 medium zucchini, sliced
1 jalapeño chili, seeded, sliced
2 tablespoons minced fresh cilantro
⅛ teaspoon cayenne pepper

1½ cups lightly packed shredded cheddar cheese (about 6 ounces)
Additional chopped fresh cilantro

For salsa roja: Heat olive oil in heavy medium saucepan over medium heat. Add onion and sauté until tender, about 6 minutes. Add garlic and cumin and continue cooking 1 minute, stirring constantly. Stir in tomatoes with their juices and chipotle chilies. Simmer until slightly thickened, stirring occasionally, about 30 minutes. Season with salt and pepper. (*Salsa can be prepared up to 2 days ahead. Cover and refrigerate.*)

For polenta: Brush 9 × 13-inch baking pan lightly with olive oil. Bring water, salt and cayenne to boil in heavy large saucepan. Gradually whisk in cornmeal. Whisk until mixture returns to boil. Reduce heat to low and cook until very thick, stirring occasionally, about 30 minutes. Remove from heat and stir in cheese. Season with salt and pepper. Spread mixture in prepared pan, smoothing top. Cool completely. (*Can be prepared up to 1 day ahead. Cover and refrigerate.*)

For vegetables: Heat 1 tablespoon olive oil in heavy large skillet over medium-high heat. Add mushrooms, garlic and cumin and cook until mush-

rooms are golden brown, stirring occasionally, about 7 minutes. Reduce heat to medium. Add zucchini and jalapeño and cook until zucchini is crisp-tender, stirring occasionally, about 6 minutes. Remove from heat. Add 2 tablespoons minced cilantro and cayenne pepper.

To assemble: Preheat oven to 375°F. Cut polenta into 3-inch squares. Cut each square diagonally into 2 triangles. Spread salsa evenly over bottom of 9 × 13-inch baking dish. Arrange polenta triangles in baking dish atop sauce in slightly overlapping rows. Spoon vegetable mixture over polenta. Sprinkle with 1½ cups cheese. (*Can be prepared 6 hours ahead. Cover and refrigerate. Bring to room temperature before continuing.*) Cover and bake until cheese bubbles and mixture is heated through, about 30 minutes. Sprinkle with chopped cilantro.

*Available at Latin American markets, specialty foods stores and some supermarkets.

Creamy Scrambled Eggs with Herbs

4 servings

6 eggs
4 ounces light cream cheese, diced
¼ cup chopped green onions
¼ cup chopped fresh basil or 2 teaspoons dried, crumbled
2 tablespoons chopped fresh parsley

2 tablespoons milk
2 teaspoons chopped fresh oregano or ½ teaspoon dried, crumbled
2 tablespoons (¼ stick) butter

Beat eggs in large bowl to blend. Beat in next 6 ingredients. Season with salt and pepper. Melt butter in heavy large skillet over medium-high heat. Add egg mixture and stir until eggs are scrambled, about 4 minutes. Serve immediately.

5 ❦ Vegetables, Grains and Breads

It's easy to forget that vegetables, grains and breads do a lot more than look pretty on a plate or add interest in terms of taste and texture to the main course. In fact, without these nutritionally important side dishes, balancing a diet would be very difficult. And steak without potatoes would get old pretty fast. You can't go wrong with simply prepared side dishes—the baked potatoes, steamed broccoli and such that most of us rely on—but you can get bored. You *won't* get bored, however, if you keep this tempting selection of recipes on hand.

Instead of baked potatoes tonight, take a look at Scalloped Potatoes with Gouda and Fennel, a creamy, cheesy casserole that cooks in about the same amount of time. And instead of ordinary steamed broccoli, how about Broccoli Puree with Parmesan and Nutmeg, which can be prepared ahead and reheated before serving?

Rice is fine, but there are times when Rice Pilaf with Spinach and White Beans—a good-for-you mix of brown rice, cannellini, spinach and pine nuts—might be better. You could also try Risotto with Radicchio and Tomatoes or Saffron Rice with Chorizo.

And while most everyone enjoys a roll or a slice of bread with dinner, you'll get double the thanks if it's warm from your oven. Make the Sweet Potato Rolls here up to a month ahead, freeze them, then rewarm just before serving. The Buttermilk Biscuits bake in just about 30 minutes, making them almost as easy as store-bought, and a whole lot fresher.

 *Vegetables*

Four-Onion Gratin

Leeks, shallots, onions and garlic combine to make a rich, delicious side dish.

8 servings

¼ cup (½ stick) butter
6 leeks (white and pale green parts only), sliced
2 large onions, cut into eighths
8 shallots, halved
2 garlic cloves, minced

1½ 10-ounce bags frozen baby onions, thawed, drained
2 cups whipping cream
2 tablespoons dry breadcrumbs
2 tablespoons chopped fresh parsley

Melt butter in heavy large skillet over medium heat. Add leeks, large onions, shallots and garlic and sauté until all are tender, about 20 minutes. Add baby onions and cook 10 minutes longer, stirring occasionally. Mix in 2 cups whipping cream. Boil until cream is thickened to sauce consistency, about 10 minutes. Transfer vegetable-cream mixture to 6-cup shallow baking dish. (*Can be prepared 1 day ahead. Cover and refrigerate. Return mixture to room temperature before continuing with recipe.*)

Preheat oven to 425°F. Sprinkle breadcrumbs over onion mixture. Bake until breadcrumbs are golden brown and onion mixture bubbles, about 20 minutes. Sprinkle gratin with parsley.

Tomatoes Vinaigrette

A side dish for grilled chicken, steak or fish.

4 servings

3 large tomatoes, chopped
¼ cup red wine vinegar
1 garlic clove, finely chopped
½ teaspoon salt
½ teaspoon dried oregano, crumbled

Pinch of sugar
Pepper
2 tablespoons olive oil (optional)
2 tablespoons chopped fresh Italian parsley

Combine first 7 ingredients in medium bowl. Mix in oil if using. Sprinkle with chopped parsley and serve immediately.

Cucumbers with Spiced Yogurt

A refreshing side dish.

4 servings

1 medium cucumber, peeled, halved lengthwise, seeded, thinly sliced
1 cup plain yogurt

1½ teaspoons minced jalapeño chili
⅛ teaspoon ground cumin
Cayenne pepper

Combine first 4 ingredients in medium bowl. Season with salt and cayenne pepper. Toss well. (*Can be prepared 4 hours ahead. Cover and refrigerate.*)

Broccoli Puree with Parmesan and Nutmeg

8 servings

3 pounds broccoli (about 2 large bunches)
6 tablespoons (¾ stick) unsalted butter, cut up

⅔ cup grated Parmesan cheese
¼ teaspoon ground nutmeg

Cut broccoli stems into 1-inch pieces. Cut tops into florets. Bring large pot of salted water to boil. Add broccoli stems and cook 6 minutes. Add broccoli florets and cook until stems and florets are very tender, about 6 more minutes. Drain well. Set aside 10 florets. Place remaining broccoli in processor. Add butter and puree, stopping occasionally to scrape down sides of bowl, about 5 minutes. Blend in grated Parmesan cheese and ground nutmeg. Season to taste with salt and pepper. (*Can be prepared 1 day ahead. Cover and refrigerate florets and puree separately. Bring florets to room temperature before continuing.*)
Reheat broccoli puree in saucepan. Garnish with broccoli florets and serve.

Stewed Cabbage and Apples

Great with chicken, fish or pork.

12 servings

3 tablespoons butter
1 medium green cabbage head, finely shredded
2 large tart green apples, peeled, cored, thinly sliced

2 large McIntosh apples, peeled, cored, thinly sliced
Generous pinch of caraway seeds
¼ cup sour cream

Melt butter in heavy large skillet over medium heat. Add cabbage, apples and caraway. Season with salt and pepper. Cook until cabbage is tender, stirring occasionally, about 8 minutes. Remove from heat and mix in sour cream. Transfer to dish and serve immediately.

Leek and Onion Sauté

6 servings

¼ cup olive oil
2 leeks, halved, sliced
2 medium red onions, halved, sliced
1 medium onion, halved, sliced
½ cup chicken stock or canned chicken broth

3 tablespoons Sherry vinegar
2 tablespoons sugar
⅛ teaspoon ground cloves

Heat oil in heavy large skillet over medium heat. Add leeks and onions. Cover and cook 10 minutes. Uncover and cook until tender, stirring occasionally, about 30 minutes. Add stock, vinegar, sugar and cloves. Simmer until liquid is syrupy, stirring constantly, about 7 minutes. Season with salt and pepper. Serve onion sauté warm or at room temperature.

Potato and Wild Mushroom Gratin

It's hard to believe that this luscious casserole is made without any cream or milk.

8 servings

2 cups chicken stock or canned broth
2 ounces dried porcini or shiitake mushrooms

6 tablespoons (¾ stick) butter
2 medium onions, chopped
3 leeks (white and pale green parts only), chopped

2 cups dry white wine
1 teaspoon dried rosemary, crumbled

4 pounds russet potatoes, peeled, thinly sliced (⅛ inch thick)

2 tablespoons (¼ stick) unsalted butter, melted
Minced fresh chives

Bring stock to simmer in medium saucepan. Add mushrooms; remove from heat. Let mushrooms soak 30 minutes to soften. Squeeze mushrooms, reserving stock. Strain stock. Chop mushrooms, discarding hard stems.

Preheat oven to 350°F. Butter 9 × 13-inch baking dish. Melt 6 tablespoons butter in heavy large skillet over medium heat. Add onions and leeks and sauté until tender but not brown, about 20 minutes. Add mushroom soaking liquid, mushrooms, wine and rosemary and bring to boil. Season with salt and pepper.

Arrange half of potatoes in prepared dish. Using slotted spoon, top potatoes with onions, leeks and mushrooms. Pour half of liquid over. Top with remaining potatoes, overlapping slices. Pour remaining liquid over. Cover tightly with foil. Bake until potatoes are almost tender, about 1 hour 15 minutes. Uncover and bake until potatoes are tender, most of liquid is absorbed and top is beginning to brown, about 45 minutes longer.

Preheat broiler. Brush top of potatoes with 2 tablespoons melted butter. Broil until golden. Sprinkle with chives and serve.

Pumpkin-Corn Pudding

4 servings

2 tablespoons (¼ stick) butter
1 cup fresh or frozen corn kernels
1 tablespoon minced garlic

2 cups (or more) milk
1 cup canned solid-pack pumpkin
1 cup cornmeal

Melt butter in heavy medium saucepan over medium heat. Add corn and garlic. Cook 3 minutes, stirring frequently. Mix in 2 cups milk and pumpkin. Bring mixture to simmer. Gradually stir in 1 cup cornmeal. Reduce heat and cook until mixture is thick, stirring constantly, about 4 minutes. Thin mixture to desired consistency with additional milk if necessary. Season pudding generously with salt and pepper and serve.

Scalloped Potatoes with Gouda and Fennel

6 servings

1 cup whipping cream
1 cup half and half
1 medium fennel bulb, trimmed, halved, thinly sliced

1 teaspoon fennel seeds, crushed
2 pounds russet potatoes, peeled
2 cups firmly packed shredded Gouda cheese (about 8 ounces)

Preheat oven to 400°F. Generously butter 8 × 8-inch glass baking dish with 2-inch-high sides. Combine cream, half and half, fresh fennel and fennel seeds in

heavy large skillet. Thinly slice potatoes and add to skillet. Bring mixture to boil over high heat, stirring frequently to separate vegetable slices. Boil 5 minutes. Season generously with salt and pepper. Transfer half of potato mixture to prepared baking dish. Sprinkle half of Gouda over. Top with remaining potato mixture. Firmly press mixture down. Sprinkle remaining Gouda over. Cover dish tightly with foil. Bake until potatoes are tender, about 40 minutes. Uncover and bake until top is golden brown, about 10 minutes longer. Let scalloped potatoes stand 10 minutes before serving.

Wild Mushroom and Bell Pepper Sauté

6 servings

¼ cup (½ stick) butter
2 small red bell peppers, cut into bite-size triangles
2 small orange bell peppers, cut into bite-size triangles
8 ounces oyster mushrooms (cut large mushrooms into thirds)

3 tablespoons fresh tarragon leaves or 2 teaspoons dried, crumbled
3 ounces soft fresh pepper-coated goat cheese, crumbled

Melt butter in heavy large skillet over medium heat. Add bell peppers and sauté until tender, about 8 minutes. Stir in mushrooms. Season to taste with salt and pepper. Sauté until mushrooms are golden brown, about 5 minutes. Mix in tarragon; cook 1 minute. Sprinkle with goat cheese and serve.

 *Grains*

Saffron Rice with Chorizo

A great side dish for chicken or fish.

6 servings

¼ cup olive oil
1 large onion, chopped
1 large red bell pepper, chopped
3 large garlic cloves, minced
2 cups long-grain rice
¾ pound smoked, fully cooked Spanish chorizo* or pepperoni, cut diagonally into ¼-inch-thick slices

4 cups canned chicken broth
¼ teaspoon (scant) saffron threads
¼ cup minced fresh parsley

Heat oil in heavy large saucepan over medium heat. Add onion, bell pepper and garlic and sauté until vegetables are tender, about 6 minutes. Add rice and stir until translucent, about 1 minute. Add sausage, broth and saffron and bring to boil, stirring occasionally. Reduce heat, cover and simmer until rice is tender, about 15 minutes. Remove from heat. Let stand 5 minutes. Season with salt and pepper. Mix in parsley and serve immediately.

*A pork link sausage flavored with garlic and spices, and milder than Mexican chorizo. Spanish chorizo is available at Spanish markets.

Seven-Vegetable Couscous with Chunky Onion Harissa

8 servings

¼ cup plus 1 tablespoon olive oil
2 large leeks (white and pale green parts only), minced
4 large garlic cloves, chopped
2¼ cups chicken stock or canned broth
1 cup raisins
1 cup butternut squash, peeled, cut into ½-inch cubes
1 large yellow crookneck squash, cut into ½-inch cubes
1 large zucchini, cut into ½-inch cubes
¾ cup frozen baby lima beans, thawed

1 teaspoon turmeric
½ teaspoon ground ginger
Large pinch cayenne pepper
1 cup diced seeded Italian plum tomatoes
¾ cup frozen peas, thawed
½ cup coarsely chopped fresh cilantro
1½ cups (about 10 ounces) couscous

Lemon wedges
Chunky Onion Harissa
(see recipe)

Heat oil in heavy large Dutch oven over low heat. Add leeks and garlic. Cover and cook until leeks are very tender, but not brown, stirring occasionally, about 10 minutes. Add chicken stock, raisins, squashes, zucchini, lima beans, turmeric, ginger and cayenne pepper. Season generously with salt and pepper. Increase heat and bring mixture to boil. Cover, reduce heat to medium and simmer until vegetables are crisp-tender, about 5 minutes. Mix in tomatoes, peas and cilantro, then couscous. Remove from heat. Cover and let stand 10 minutes.

Fluff couscous with fork. Transfer to large platter. Garnish with lemon wedges. Serve, passing Chunky Onion Harissa separately.

Chunky Onion Harissa

Traditional harissa is a smooth and fiery pepper sauce. This version is spicy and salsalike, with a crunchy texture.

Makes about 2 cups

¼ cup tomato paste
1 tablespoon plus 1 teaspoon dried crushed red pepper
¾ teaspoon cayenne pepper
1 cup olive oil

½ cup red wine vinegar
6 green onions, chopped
1 small red onion, chopped
2 large garlic cloves, minced

Combine tomato paste, crushed red pepper and cayenne pepper in medium bowl. Gradually whisk in olive oil. Whisk in vinegar. Mix in onions and garlic. Season generously with salt and pepper. (*Can be prepared 8 hours ahead. Let stand at room temperature. Stir harissa well before using.*)

Lima Bean Risotto

6 servings

3 tablespoons butter
1 small onion, chopped
2 fresh rosemary sprigs or
   1½ teaspoons dried, crumbled

3 14½-ounce cans chicken broth
1½ cups (about) water

2¼ cups Arborio rice*
¾ cup dry white wine
1½ 10-ounce packages frozen baby
   lima beans, thawed
1¼ cups grated Parmesan cheese

Melt butter in heavy medium saucepan over medium heat. Add onion and rosemary and cook until onion is translucent, stirring occasionally, about 8 minutes.

Meanwhile, bring chicken broth and 1½ cups water to simmer in medium saucepan. Reduce heat to very low and keep mixture hot.

Add rice to onion mixture and stir 2 minutes. Add wine and stir until all liquid is absorbed. Add lima beans and ¾ cup broth mixture; reduce heat and simmer until liquid is absorbed, stirring frequently. Continue adding enough of remaining broth mixture ½ cup at a time until rice is just tender but still firm to bite, stirring frequently and allowing each addition to be absorbed before adding next, about 20 minutes. Remove risotto from heat. Mix in grated Parmesan. Season risotto to taste with salt and pepper and serve.

*Arborio is an Italian short-grain rice. It is available at Italian markets, specialty foods stores and some supermarkets. Medium-grain rice can be substituted.

Rice Pilaf with Spinach and White Beans

"Polishing," which removes the hull, bran and most of the germ, makes rice more digestible but strips it of much nutritional value. The long-grain brown variety called for here has the outer bran layer intact, and it offers fiber, vitamins, minerals and five grams of protein per cup. Besides that, brown rice can also help lower blood pressure.

4 servings

1 tablespoon olive oil
1 onion, chopped
2 garlic cloves, minced
1½ cups long-grain brown rice
3 cups canned low-salt chicken
   broth

2 15-ounce cans cannellini (white
   kidney beans), rinsed, drained

2 10-ounce packages frozen leaf
   spinach, thawed, drained
½ cup grated Parmesan cheese
3 tablespoons pine nuts, lightly
   toasted
4 oil-packed sun-dried tomatoes,
   drained, thinly sliced

Heat oil in heavy large saucepan over medium-high heat. Add onion and garlic and sauté until onion is golden brown, about 10 minutes. Reduce heat to medium-low. Stir in rice. Cook until grains become opaque, stirring constantly, about 3 minutes. Add broth and bring to simmer. Cover and cook until rice is tender, about 45 minutes.

Mix in beans, spinach and Parmesan. Cover and continue cooking until heated through, about 3 minutes. Season with salt and pepper. Transfer to serving dish. Garnish rice pilaf with pine nuts and sun-dried tomatoes.

Risotto with Radicchio and Tomatoes

4 servings

8 cups water
1½ cups Arborio rice*

2 tablespoons olive oil
1 garlic clove, chopped
1 small radicchio head, shredded

1 14-ounce can Italian plum tomatoes, drained, chopped, juices reserved
1 cup whipping cream
½ cup chicken stock or canned broth
Grated Parmesan cheese

Bring water to boil in heavy large saucepan over medium-high heat. Add rice and cook until tender but still firm to bite, stirring frequently, about 12 minutes. Drain. (*Rice can be prepared 2 days ahead. Cover and refrigerate.*)

Heat oil in heavy large saucepan over medium heat. Add garlic and sauté 30 seconds. Add radicchio and sauté until just wilted, about 2 minutes. Stir in tomatoes and their juice and simmer until liquid is slightly reduced, stirring occasionally, about 8 minutes. Add cream and stock and simmer 5 minutes. Stir in rice. Reduce heat and simmer until liquid is absorbed, stirring frequently, about 4 minutes. Season with salt and pepper. Transfer to dish. Serve, passing grated Parmesan cheese separately.

*Arborio is an Italian short-grain rice. It is available at Italian markets, specialty foods stores and some supermarkets. Medium-grain rice can be substituted.

Mixed-Grain and Vegetable Stir-Fry

Kashi is a mixture of whole oats, rye, brown rice, wheat berries, buckwheat, barley, triticale and sesame seeds. All the grains retain their fiber, bran and germ, and are an excellent source of protein, fiber, carbohydrates and minerals, with only 35 calories per ounce. Kashi is available either uncooked or as a ready-to-eat breakfast cereal. Here, the uncooked variety is used in a stir-fry with vegetables.

6 servings

Mixed Grains
1 tablespoon vegetable oil
½ cup chopped onion
1 large garlic clove, minced
1 tablespoon curry powder
1 cup Kashi or other uncooked mixed-grain cereal
½ cup lentils
1 2-inch piece cinnamon stick
2 14½-ounce cans low-salt chicken broth

Vegetables
2 tablespoons vegetable oil

1 tablespoon minced fresh ginger
2 garlic cloves, minced
4 cups broccoli florets (about 1 large bunch)
2 cups sliced carrots (about 3)
2 tablespoons water
2 red bell peppers, cut into ¼-inch-thick strips
2 cups sliced mushrooms
1 cup sliced green onions (about 4)
1 tablespoon plus 1 teaspoon low-sodium soy sauce
2 teaspoons oriental sesame oil

For grains: Heat oil in heavy large saucepan over medium-low heat. Add onion and garlic and sauté until onion is just golden brown, about 6 minutes. Add curry powder and sauté until fragrant, about 1 minute. Mix in Kashi, lentils and cinnamon stick. Stir until grains are lightly coated with oil, about 2 minutes. Add broth and bring to boil. Cover and cook until grains are tender and liquid is absorbed, about 35 minutes. Remove from heat. Season with salt. Keep warm.

For vegetables: Heat 1 tablespoon oil in wok or heavy large skillet over high heat. Add ginger and garlic and cook until just golden, stirring constantly, about 10 seconds. Add broccoli and carrots and stir-fry 1 minute. Reduce heat to medium. Add water, cover and cook until carrots are almost crisp-tender, about 3 minutes. Turn heat to high. Add remaining 1 tablespoon oil, red bell peppers, mushrooms and green onions. Stir-fry until vegetables are heated through, about 2 minutes. Remove from heat. Add soy sauce and sesame oil and toss.

Transfer grains to platter. Spoon vegetables over and serve.

 Breads

Sweet Potato Rolls

Makes 3 dozen

1½ **pounds sweet potatoes, peeled, quartered**

2 **envelopes fast-rising yeast**
¼ **cup sugar**
1½ **cups (3 sticks) unsalted butter, melted**
1 **cup honey**

¼ **cup vegetable oil**
2 **eggs, beaten to blend**
2 **teaspoons salt**
3 **cups all purpose flour**
4 **cups (about) whole wheat flour**

4 **cups graham cracker crumbs**

Cook potatoes in large saucepan of simmering water until tender, about 20 minutes. Drain, reserving 1 cup cooking liquid. Place potatoes in medium bowl. Transfer reserved cooking liquid to large bowl; cool to 120°F to 130°F.

Sprinkle yeast and sugar over reserved warm liquid; stir to dissolve. Let yeast mixture stand until foamy, about 5 minutes. Combine potatoes, ½ cup melted butter, ½ cup honey, oil, eggs and salt in processor. Blend until smooth. Add to yeast mixture. Mix in all purpose flour. Gradually stir in enough whole wheat flour ½ cup at a time to form soft, slightly sticky dough. Turn dough out onto lightly floured surface and knead until smooth and elastic, adding more whole wheat flour if sticky.

Lightly oil large bowl. Add dough, turning to coat entire surface. Cover bowl with kitchen towel. Let dough rise in warm draft-free area until doubled in volume, about 30 minutes.

Preheat oven to 400°F. Grease three 9-inch-diameter cake pans. Punch dough down. Turn dough out onto lightly floured surface and knead until smooth. Divide dough into thirds. Cut each third into 12 pieces. Roll each piece into ball. Mix remaining 1 cup melted butter and ½ cup honey until well blended. Dip each dough ball into honey mixture and then roll in graham cracker crumbs to coat. Place 12 balls in each prepared pan, arranging close together. Let stand 10 minutes. Bake until golden brown, about 25 minutes. (*Rolls can be prepared ahead. Cool completely. Wrap tightly and refrigerate 1 day or freeze up to 1 month. Reheat rolls before serving.*) Serve warm.

Prune-Sour Cream Muffins

Makes 12

Topping
2 tablespoons sugar
2 tablespoons finely chopped walnuts
¼ teaspoon ground cinnamon

Batter
2 cups all purpose flour
1¼ cups sugar
2 teaspoons baking powder
1 teaspoon baking soda
¾ teaspoon salt
1 cup chopped dried pitted prunes
½ cup chopped walnuts (about 2 ounces)
1 large egg
1 large egg yolk
1 cup sour cream
6 tablespoons (¾ stick) unsalted butter, melted
2 tablespoons milk
1 teaspoon vanilla extract

For topping: Mix all ingredients together in small bowl. Set aside.

For batter: Preheat oven to 400°F. Butter twelve ½-cup muffin cups or line with paper liners. Sift first 5 ingredients into large bowl. Add prunes and walnuts. Stir to combine. Whisk egg and yolk together in medium bowl. Add sour cream, butter, milk and vanilla. Stir until smooth. Make well in center of flour mixture. Add egg mixture and stir until just combined. Divide batter among prepared cups. Sprinkle each with topping. Bake until tester inserted into centers comes out clean, about 25 minutes. Turn muffins out onto rack and cool slightly before serving.

Sticky Cinnamon Rolls

Makes about 15

1½ cups all purpose flour
1 cup whole wheat flour
¼ cup firmly packed brown sugar
1 envelope rapid-rise yeast
½ teaspoon salt
½ teaspoon ground cinnamon
¾ cup warm water (125°F to 130°F)
¼ cup (½ stick) butter, melted
1 egg
1½ cups firmly packed brown sugar
1 cup (2 sticks) butter, room temperature
1 cup chopped walnuts
1 tablespoon ground cinnamon
½ cup raisins

Using electric mixer fitted with dough hook or paddle, mix first 6 ingredients in large bowl. Add water, butter and egg and mix until smooth dough forms, about 4 minutes. Transfer dough to greased bowl. Cover with plastic and clean towel. Let rise in warm draft-free area until doubled, about 30 minutes.

Butter 9 × 13-inch baking dish. Bring 1 cup brown sugar and ½ cup butter to boil in heavy small saucepan. Boil 1 minute. Remove from heat and stir in ½ cup walnuts. Pour into prepared dish. Punch dough down. Roll out on lightly floured surface to 15 × 9-inch rectangle. Spread dough evenly with remaining ½ cup butter. Sprinkle with remaining ½ cup brown sugar and 1 tablespoon cinnamon. Sprinkle with remaining ½ cup walnuts and raisins. Roll up jelly roll style, starting at 1 long side. Slice dough into 1-inch-thick rounds.

Arrange dough slices cut side down in prepared dish, spacing evenly. Cover with plastic. Let rise in warm draft-free area until doubled, about 45 minutes.

Preheat oven to 350°F. Bake rolls until golden brown, about 45 minutes. Let stand 5 minutes. Turn out onto platter. Cool slightly. Serve warm.

Buttermilk Biscuits

Makes about 20

2⅓ cups all purpose flour
3 tablespoons sugar
1 tablespoon plus 1 teaspoon cornstarch
1 tablespoon baking powder

¼ teaspoon salt
¼ cup (½ stick) unsalted butter, cut into 8 pieces
¾ cup buttermilk
1 egg

Preheat oven to 375°F. Line large cookie sheet with parchment paper. Sift first 5 ingredients into large bowl. Cut in butter using pastry blender or fingers until mixture resembles fine meal. Beat buttermilk and egg in small bowl to blend. Add buttermilk mixture to dry ingredients and mix until just combined.

Roll dough out on lightly floured surface to 1-inch-thick round. Cut out biscuits using floured 2-inch-diameter biscuit cutter. Gather and reroll scraps. Cut out additional rounds. Transfer to prepared cookie sheet spacing 1 inch apart. Bake until golden brown, about 30 minutes. Cool biscuits slightly.

Creamed Scones

Makes about 11

2½ cups all purpose flour
5 teaspoons baking powder
5 tablespoons sugar
3 tablespoons chilled unsalted butter, cut into pieces
½ cup milk

¼ cup whipping cream
1 egg yolk
⅓ cup dried currants
1 egg, beaten to blend (glaze)
Butter
Assorted jams

Preheat oven to 450°F. Lightly grease heavy large cookie sheet. Sift flour and baking powder into medium bowl. Mix in sugar. Add butter and rub with fingertips until mixture resembles fine meal. Whisk milk, whipping cream and egg yolk in small bowl to blend. Add to dry ingredients and stir just until combined. Mix in currants. Turn dough out onto floured work surface. Press to thickness of 1 inch. Cut out rounds using 2- to 2½-inch round cookie cutter. Gather scraps and press together to thickness of 1 inch. Cut out additional rounds. Transfer rounds to prepared cookie sheet, spacing evenly. Brush with glaze. Bake until golden brown, about 15 minutes. Transfer scones to racks and cool slightly. Serve warm with butter and assorted jams.

Banana-Macadamia Nut Muffins

A moist and flavorful banana-nut muffin with a distinctly tropical twist.

Makes 12

1½ cups unbleached all purpose flour
1½ teaspoons baking soda
¼ teaspoon salt
⅛ teaspoon ground nutmeg
1¼ cups mashed ripe bananas (about 3 large)
½ cup sugar

¼ cup firmly packed dark brown sugar
½ cup (1 stick) unsalted butter, melted
¼ cup milk
1 large egg
1 cup unsalted macadamia nuts, toasted, chopped

Preheat oven to 350°F. Grease 12 muffin cups or line with muffin papers. Sift first 4 ingredients into large bowl. Combine bananas, both sugars, butter, milk and egg in medium bowl. Mix into dry ingredients. Fold in half of nuts. Divide batter among prepared muffin cups. Sprinkle tops of muffins with remaining macadamia nuts. Bake until muffins are golden brown and tester inserted into center comes out clean, about 25 minutes. Transfer to rack and cool.

Quick Anadama Bread

Here's an easy baking powder version of the traditional yeast-leavened cornmeal and molasses bread. Buttermilk, instead of water, gives the loaf moistness and tang.

Makes 1 loaf

1¼ cups all purpose flour
1¼ cups whole wheat flour
½ cup yellow cornmeal
2 teaspoons baking powder
¾ teaspoon salt
½ teaspoon baking soda

1⅓ cups buttermilk
⅓ cup dark molasses
¼ cup (½ stick) butter, melted
1 egg
Poppy seeds

Preheat oven to 350°F. Grease 9 × 5-inch glass loaf pan. Mix all purpose flour, whole wheat flour, yellow cornmeal, baking powder, salt and baking soda in large bowl. Combine buttermilk, dark molasses, butter and egg in another bowl and mix to blend. Add to dry ingredients and stir until just blended. Spoon into prepared loaf pan. Sprinkle with poppy seeds. Bake until loaf is springy to touch, about 1 hour. Cool in pan on rack 10 minutes. Turn out onto rack. Cool bread to room temperature. Cut into slices and serve.

Blueberry-Lemon Bread

Makes one 8-inch loaf

1½ cups all purpose flour
1 teaspoon baking powder
¼ teaspoon salt
6 tablespoons (¾ stick) unsalted butter, room temperature
1⅓ cups sugar

2 large eggs
2 teaspoons grated lemon peel
½ cup milk
1½ cups fresh blueberries or frozen, thawed, drained

3 tablespoons fresh lemon juice

Preheat oven to 325°F. Butter 8½ × 4½ × 2½-inch loaf pan. Combine first 3 ingredients in small bowl. Using electric mixer, cream butter with 1 cup sugar in large bowl until mixture is light and fluffy. Add eggs 1 at a time, beating well after each addition. Add lemon peel. Mix in dry ingredients alternately with milk, beginning and ending with dry ingredients. Fold in blueberries. Spoon batter into prepared loaf pan. Bake until golden brown and toothpick inserted into center comes out clean, about 1 hour 15 minutes.

Meanwhile, bring remaining ⅓ cup sugar and lemon juice to boil in small saucepan, stirring until sugar dissolves.

Pierce top of hot loaf several times with toothpick. Pour hot lemon mixture over loaf in pan. Cool 30 minutes in pan on rack. Turn bread out of pan and cool completely on rack before serving.

6 🍎 Desserts

Not an issue of *Bon Appétit* goes by that we don't feature desserts in at least one section of the magazine, and you can imagine how difficult it was to choose the best of the many sinfully tempting sweets we ran during the course of the year. But we did, and for all you loyal sweet tooths out there, here they are, both simple and extravagant, light and decadent, classic and contemporary.

Fruit desserts are always popular, and it's easy to see why with such appealing recipes as Apple and Raisin Crisp, Individual Pear and Maple Cobblers and Broiled Figs with Oranges and Sherry Cream. If custards and puddings are your idea of heaven, be sure to try one of our cover recipes, English Chocolate Trifle with Apricots and Raspberries. Also irresistible are White Chocolate Crème Brûlée and Layered Chocolate and Caramel Mousse. For all the ice cream lovers, there is a big selection of frozen desserts, among them an outrageously rich Coffee-Molasses Ice Cream with Molasses-glazed Pecans.

For the bakers, there are down-home pies, delicate tarts and lovely pastries, including Chocolate Date-Nut Baklava. The cakes featured here run the gamut from simple cheesecakes to the drop-dead gorgeous Lemon-Lattice White Chocolate Cake.

The chapter—and the recipe section of the book—ends on a final sweet note: cookies and brownies. Here you'll find Old-fashioned Sugar Cookies, Island Macaroons, Double Chocolate Brownies, to name just a few of the temptations—in case we hadn't gotten your attention yet.

 Fruit Desserts

Apple and Raisin Crisp

Nothing more than fruit baked with a crumbly nut, flour, sugar and butter topping, this crisp is as simple to make as it is delicious.

8 servings

Topping
1¼ cups old-fashioned oats
1 cup plus 2 tablespoons firmly packed brown sugar
¾ cup all purpose flour
½ teaspoon ground cinnamon
¼ teaspoon salt
¾ cup (1½ sticks) unsalted butter, room temperature
¾ cup walnuts, chopped

Filling
4 pounds pippin or Granny Smith apples, peeled, cored, sliced
1½ cups golden brown raisins
½ cup sugar
1 tablespoon fresh lemon juice
1 tablespoon all purpose flour
¾ teaspoon ground cinnamon
Vanilla ice cream

Preheat oven to 375°F. Butter 9 × 13½-inch glass baking dish.
For topping: Mix first 5 ingredients in large bowl. Add butter and rub into mixture until coarse crumbs form. Mix in walnuts.
For filling: Combine first 6 ingredients in large bowl. Mix well to blend.
Transfer filling to prepared dish. Spread topping over. Bake until topping is golden brown, about 55 minutes. Serve warm with ice cream.

Broiled Figs with Oranges and Sherry Cream

6 servings

1 cup chilled whipping cream
3 tablespoons golden brown sugar
3 tablespoons cream Sherry

6 oranges, peeled, white pith removed, sliced into rounds

Chopped fresh mint
12 fresh figs, halved lengthwise
Golden brown sugar
Cream Sherry

Whip cream with 3 tablespoons brown sugar to soft peaks. Add 3 tablespoons Sherry and beat to firm peaks. Cover and chill. (*Can be prepared 6 hours ahead.*)
Preheat broiler. Arrange oranges in ring around center of each plate. Top with mint. Arrange figs cut side up in broilerproof pan. Sprinkle with brown sugar and Sherry. Broil until sugar begins to caramelize. Mound cream in center of each plate. Top with figs and serve.

Poached Pear Sundaes

2 servings

2 cups water
½ cup honey
2 small strips orange peel (orange part only)
2 pears, peeled, halved, cored

Vanilla ice cream
Chocolate syrup
Whipped cream
Grated semisweet chocolate

Bring water, honey and orange peel to boil in heavy medium saucepan. Add pears. Cover and simmer over medium-low heat until pears are tender but still

firm, about 12 minutes. Refrigerate pears in poaching liquid until cold, about 3 hours. (*Pears can be prepared 1 day ahead.*)

Slice pears. Arrange slices in 2 dishes. Top with 1 scoop vanilla ice cream. Drizzle chocolate syrup over. Garnish with whipped cream and chocolate.

Peaches and Raspberries in Spiced White Wine

8 servings

1 bottle (750 ml) Italian dry white wine, such as Pinot Bianco or Pinot Grigio
½ cup sugar
4 ¾ × 2-inch orange peel strips (orange part only)

3 cinnamon sticks

6 peaches
2 ½-pint baskets raspberries
Biscotti

Combine 1 cup wine, sugar, orange peel and cinnamon in small saucepan. Stir over low heat until sugar dissolves. Increase heat; simmer 15 minutes. Remove from heat; add remaining wine.

Blanch peaches in large pot of boiling water 20 seconds. Transfer to bowl of cold water, using slotted spoon. Drain. Pull off skin with small sharp knife. Slice peaches and transfer to large bowl. Add raspberries and wine mixture. Cover and refrigerate at least 1 hour. (*Can be prepared 6 hours ahead. Stir occasionally.*) Divide fruit and wine among glass goblets. Serve with biscotti.

Triple-Ginger Peach Crisp

8 servings

Topping
¾ cup slivered blanched almonds
⅓ cup firmly packed golden brown sugar
15 purchased gingersnaps, broken into pieces
1 cup quick-cooking oats
1 teaspoon ground ginger
¾ teaspoon salt
½ cup plus 2 tablespoons (1¼ sticks) chilled unsalted butter, cut into pieces
2 large egg yolks

5 tablespoons chopped crystallized ginger

Filling
2 tablespoons fresh lemon juice
4 pounds ripe peaches (about 10 peaches)
½ cup firmly packed golden brown sugar
2 tablespoons cornstarch
1 large egg yolk
Vanilla ice cream

Preheat oven to 375°F. Butter 13 × 9 × 2-inch baking dish.

For topping: Chop almonds with sugar in processor using on/off turns. Add gingersnaps and process until coarsely chopped. Blend in oats, ground ginger and salt. Add butter and cut in using on/off turns until coarse meal forms. Add egg yolks and chopped crystallized ginger and process until ingredients are combined but mixture is still chunky.

For filling: Place lemon juice in large bowl. Peel and pit peaches. Thinly slice into bowl; toss to coat with lemon juice. Mix in sugar, cornstarch and yolk.

Spoon peach mixture into prepared dish. Sprinkle topping evenly over peach filling. Bake until topping is deep golden brown, about 1 hour. Let dessert cool at least 15 minutes. Serve warm with ice cream.

Individual Pear and Maple Cobblers

6 servings

Filling

3 pounds ripe Bartlett pears, peeled, quartered, cored
⅔ cup pure maple syrup
1 tablespoon plus 2 teaspoons all purpose flour
½ teaspoon vanilla extract
⅛ teaspoon (generous) ground nutmeg
1½ tablespoons butter

Topping
1½ cups all purpose flour
2¼ teaspoons baking powder
¼ teaspoon ground nutmeg
6 tablespoons (¾ stick) chilled unsalted butter, cut into ½-inch pieces
9 tablespoons half and half
9 tablespoons pure maple syrup
¾ teaspoon vanilla extract

Melted butter
Sugar
Ground nutmeg

1 cup chilled whipping cream
Additional pure maple syrup

For filling: Preheat oven to 425°F. Cut pears crosswise into ¼-inch-thick slices. Combine in large bowl with maple syrup, flour, vanilla extract and ground nutmeg. Divide among six ⅔-cup custard cups or soufflé dishes. Dot tops with butter. Bake filling until hot and bubbling, about 18 minutes.

Meanwhile prepare topping: Mix first 3 ingredients in processor. Add 6 tablespoons chilled butter and cut in until mixture resembles fine meal. Transfer to large bowl. Mix half and half, 6 tablespoons syrup and vanilla in another bowl. Add to dry ingredients and stir until just combined.

Working quickly, drop batter in 3 mounds, 1 heaping tablespoon per mound, atop hot filling in each cup. Brush topping with melted butter and sprinkle with sugar and nutmeg. Immediately return cups to oven and bake 8 minutes. Reduce temperature to 375°F and bake until toppings are golden and just firm to touch, about 14 minutes. Let cool at least 15 minutes.

In medium bowl, beat 1 cup chilled whipping cream with 3 tablespoons maple syrup to soft peaks. Serve cobblers warm with whipped cream. Drizzle additional maple syrup over.

❦ *Custards, Puddings and Mousses*

Chocolate Almond Pâté

10 servings

1¼ cups whipping cream
¼ cup (½ stick) unsalted butter
1 pound bittersweet (not unsweetened) or semisweet chocolate, chopped
1 cup ground toasted almonds
1 teaspoon almond extract

Whipped cream
Whole toasted almonds
Fresh mint sprigs

Line 7½ × 3½ × 2¼-inch loaf pan with waxed paper. Bring cream and butter to simmer in heavy medium saucepan over medium heat. Reduce heat to low. Add chocolate and stir until melted and smooth. Remove from heat and stir in

ground almonds and extract. Pour into prepared pan. Cover and chill overnight. (*Can be prepared up to 2 days ahead.*)

To unmold, turn loaf pan out onto work surface. Peel off waxed paper. Cut pâté into thin slices with warm thin-bladed knife. Place pâté slices on plates. Garnish with rosettes of whipped cream, whole almonds and mint.

English Chocolate Trifle with Apricots and Raspberries (Cover Recipe)

16 servings

White Chocolate Pudding
  10 large egg yolks
  ⅓ cup sugar
  2 tablespoons cornstarch
  4 cups half and half
  1 pound imported white chocolate (such as Lindt), chopped
  ½ cup (1 stick) unsalted butter, cut into pieces

Poached Apricots
  ⅔ cup plus 3 tablespoons water
  ⅓ cup honey
  ⅓ cup sugar
  4 tablespoons fresh lemon juice
  9 ounces dried apricots (about 2 cups)

Dark Chocolate Cream
  ½ cup whipping cream
  5 tablespoons light corn syrup
  4 ounces bittersweet (not unsweetened) or semisweet chocolate, chopped

  1½ (about) 12-ounce pound cakes
  6 tablespoons dark rum
  3 tablespoons white crème de cacao liqueur
  4 ½-pint baskets fresh raspberries or 16 ounces frozen unsweetened raspberries, thawed

  Firmly whipped cream

For pudding: Whisk yolks, sugar and cornstarch in medium bowl. Bring half and half to simmer in heavy large saucepan. Gradually whisk hot half and half into yolk mixture. Return mixture to same saucepan and whisk over medium heat until custard boils. Boil 1 minute, whisking constantly. Remove from heat. Pour pudding into large bowl. Add white chocolate and butter and whisk until melted and smooth. Refrigerate pudding until thick and cold, whisking occasionally, approximately 3 hours.

For apricots: Line cookie sheet with foil. Brush lightly with vegetable oil. Combine ⅔ cup water, honey, sugar and 2 tablespoons lemon juice in heavy medium saucepan. Stir over high heat until sugar dissolves. Add apricots and bring to boil. Reduce heat, cover and simmer 10 minutes.

Transfer 5 apricots and ¼ cup poaching syrup to heavy small skillet. Combine remaining apricots with remaining poaching syrup, 3 tablespoons water and 2 tablespoons lemon juice in processor and puree. Pour puree into bowl. Cook apricots in skillet over high heat until syrup is reduced to a glaze, turning apricots once, about 4 minutes. Using tongs, transfer candied apricots to foil. Cool. Mix remaining syrup into puree. (*Can be prepared 1 day ahead. Cover candied apricots and puree separately and let stand at room temperature.*)

For dark chocolate cream: Bring cream and corn syrup to simmer in heavy medium saucepan. Reduce heat to low. Add chocolate and whisk until melted. Refrigerate until cold but still pourable, stirring occasionally, about 30 minutes.

Cut cakes into ½-inch-thick slices. Cut each slice into 4 squares. Arrange enough cake in 4-quart glass trifle dish to cover bottom, fitting tightly. Mix rum and crème de cacao in small bowl. Drizzle 3 tablespoons rum mixture over cake. Drop ⅓ of apricot puree by spoonfuls over cake. Gently spread with back of spoon, allowing puree to show at sides of bowl. Sprinkle 1¼ baskets berries over, arranging some berries to show at sides of bowl. Starting 1 inch in from sides of

bowl, pour ⅓ of dark chocolate cream over, making sure it does not touch sides of bowl. Starting at edge, pour 2 cups white chocolate pudding over chocolate cream. Repeat layering with remaining cake, rum mixture, apricot puree, raspberries, dark chocolate cream and white chocolate pudding in 2 more layers each. Smooth top. Cover and refrigerate overnight.

Spoon whipped cream into pastry bag fitted with medium star tip. Pipe 8 rosettes of cream around edge of trifle, spacing evenly. Decorate with candied apricots and remaining berries. (*Can be prepared 8 hours ahead. Cover and refrigerate.*) Serve trifle cold.

Cherry Crème Brûlée

Sugar-topped cherries crown a smooth custard in this inventive dessert.

6 servings

Custard
- 5 large egg yolks
- ⅓ cup sugar
- 1½ cups whipping cream
- ¼ cup milk
- ¼ teaspoon ground cinnamon

Cherries
- 10 ounces cherries, halved, pitted
- 6 teaspoons raw sugar* or golden brown sugar

For custard: Preheat oven to 325°F. Beat yolks and sugar in large bowl to combine. Whisk in remaining ingredients. Divide mixture among six ⅔-cup ramekins or custard cups. Place in large baking pan. Add enough water to pan to come ¾ inch up sides of ramekins. Bake until custards are gently set, about 1 hour. Remove from water. Cover and refrigerate until well chilled, about 6 hours. (*Can be prepared 3 days ahead.*)

For cherries: Place cherries in heavy medium nonstick saucepan. Cover and cook over low heat until tender, stirring often, about 8 minutes. Cool.

Preheat broiler. Spoon cherries atop custard in ramekins. Sprinkle 1 teaspoon raw sugar over each. Broil until sugar melts and bubbles, about 1 minute. Cool crème brûlées slightly and serve.

*Raw sugar, also known as Demerara or turbinado sugar, is available at most supermarkets and also at natural foods stores.

Lemon Soufflés

8 servings

- 1 cup milk
- 7 tablespoons sugar
- 1 tablespoon grated lemon peel

- 3 egg yolks
- ¼ cup fresh lemon juice
- 3 tablespoons all purpose flour

- Additional sugar (for dusting cups)
- 6 large egg whites
  Pinch of salt
- 2 tablespoons kirsch (clear cherry brandy) or other brandy
  Powdered sugar

Bring milk, 6 tablespoons sugar and lemon peel to boil in heavy medium saucepan, stirring occasionally. Remove from heat and let stand 20 minutes.

Whisk yolks and lemon juice in medium bowl to blend. Add flour and whisk until smooth. Whisk in milk mixture. Return mixture to saucepan and bring to boil, stirring frequently. Continue boiling 1 minute, stirring constantly. Transfer to medium bowl. Press plastic wrap onto surface of lemon pastry cream and cool. (*Can be prepared 3 days ahead. Cover and refrigerate.*)

Preheat oven to 400°F. Butter eight ½- to ⅔-cup soufflé dishes or custard cups. Dust with sugar. Place on cookie sheet. Beat egg whites with salt in large bowl to soft peaks. Add remaining 1 tablespoon sugar and beat until medium-stiff peaks form. Mix kirsch into lemon pastry cream. Fold in ⅓ of whites. Gently fold in remaining whites. Divide mixture among prepared dishes. Bake until soufflés puff and tops brown, about 17 minutes. Sift powdered sugar over tops of soufflés and serve immediately.

New Mexico Bread Pudding

10 to 12 servings

1 cup raisins	6 tablespoons (¾ stick) unsalted butter, melted
¼ cup bourbon	
11 ounces day-old white bread, cut into ½-inch pieces (about 11 cups)	3 large eggs
	1 teaspoon ground cinnamon
	½ teaspoon ground nutmeg
2½ cups whipping cream	1⅓ cups chopped pecans (about 5½ ounces)
2½ cups applesauce	
1⅓ cups sugar	1 cup pine nuts (about 5½ ounces)
	Vanilla ice cream

Combine raisins and bourbon in small bowl. Let stand 1 hour. Drain.

Preheat oven to 350°F. Generously butter 11 × 9 × 2-inch baking pan. Place bread in pan. Whisk cream, applesauce, sugar, butter, eggs, cinnamon and nutmeg in large bowl to blend. Mix in raisins, pecans and pine nuts. Pour over bread in pan. Cover with foil. Bake until center of pudding is firm, about 1 hour. Cool slightly. Spoon pudding into bowls. Top with ice cream.

Layered Chocolate and Caramel Mousse

The alternating layers of chocolate and caramel mousse look very elegant in a simple stemmed glass.

8 servings

Caramel Mousse
- ¾ cup whipping cream
- ¾ cup sugar
- 5 tablespoons water
- 3 tablespoons unsalted butter, room temperature
- 1¼ cups chilled whipping cream
- 1 teaspoon vanilla extract

Chocolate Mousse
- 5 ounces semisweet chocolate, chopped
- 1½ cups chilled whipping cream
- ½ cup powdered sugar
- 3 tablespoons unsweetened cocoa powder
- 1 tablespoon dark rum
- 1 teaspoon vanilla extract

For caramel mousse: Heat ¾ cup whipping cream in heavy small saucepan to lukewarm. Remove from heat. Mix sugar with 5 tablespoons water in heavy medium saucepan over medium heat until sugar dissolves. Increase heat and boil without stirring until sugar turns deep golden brown, occasionally swirling pan and washing down sides with wet pastry brush, about 8 minutes. Add warm whipping cream (mixture will bubble up) and cook over low heat until mixture is smooth, stirring constantly. Mix in 3 tablespoons unsalted butter. Pour caramel into small bowl. Cover and refrigerate until cold, about 2 hours.

Beat 1¼ cups chilled whipping cream and 1 teaspoon vanilla extract to soft peaks in large bowl. Reserve 3 tablespoons caramel for topping. Fold remaining caramel into whipped cream. Cover and refrigerate.

For chocolate mousse: Melt 5 ounces semisweet chocolate in large bowl set over saucepan of simmering water, stirring until chocolate is smooth. Cool to lukewarm stirring occasionally. Using electric mixer, beat chilled whipping cream, powdered sugar, unsweetened cocoa powder, dark rum and vanilla extract in another large bowl until stiff peaks form. Whisk ¾ cup of cream mixture into melted chocolate. Fold remaining cream mixture into chocolate.

Spoon half of chocolate mousse in bottom of 8 large (10- to 12-ounce) clear stemmed glasses; smooth surface of each. Spoon half of caramel mousse over, spreading to edge of each glass. Repeat chocolate and caramel mousse layers. Drizzle some of 3 tablespoons reserved caramel over each. Cover and refrigerate at least 4 hours. (*Can be prepared 1 day ahead.*)

Raspberry Charlotte Russe

12 servings

Charlotte
2 7-ounce packages Champagne biscuits (4-inch-long ladyfingers)
4 teaspoons unflavored gelatin
1¼ cups milk (do not use lowfat or nonfat)
1 cup whipping cream
1 vanilla bean, split lengthwise
8 large egg yolks
1 cup sugar
2 tablespoons raspberry liqueur

1 cup chilled whipping cream
1 cup sour cream
1½ ½-pint baskets raspberries or 2 cups frozen unsweetened raspberries, thawed, drained

Sauce
2 10-ounce packages frozen raspberries in syrup, thawed
2 tablespoons sugar
2 tablespoons kirsch (clear cherry brandy) (optional)

Additional fresh raspberries

For charlotte: Place 4 ladyfingers rounded sides down in bottom of 9-inch-diameter springform pan, dividing pan into fourths. Cut and trim several ladyfingers to fit inside each fourth; place rounded sides down and space evenly. Trim remaining ladyfingers to 2½-inch-long pieces. Place rounded sides facing out around sides of pan with rounded ends pointing toward base of pan.

Sprinkle gelatin over ¼ cup milk in small bowl. Let stand until softened, about 5 minutes. Scald remaining 1 cup milk with 1 cup cream and vanilla bean in heavy large saucepan. Remove vanilla bean and reserve. Using electric mixer, beat yolks with sugar in medium bowl until pale yellow and slowly dissolving ribbon forms when beaters are lifted. Gradually beat warm cream mixture into yolk mixture. Return mixture to saucepan. Stir over medium-low heat until custard thickens slightly, about 6 minutes; do not boil. Pour into bowl. Add gelatin mixture and stir until dissolved. Mix in raspberry liqueur. Let custard stand until cool but not set, stirring frequently, about 20 minutes.

Place 1 cup chilled whipping cream and sour cream in large bowl. Scrape in seeds from vanilla bean; discard pod. Using electric mixer, beat mixture until stiff. Fold cream mixture into custard. Pour half of mixture into prepared pan. Sprinkle berries over. Pour remaining mixture over. Cover and chill overnight.

For sauce: Puree thawed raspberries in processor. Strain through sieve to remove seeds. Mix in sugar and kirsch. Cover and refrigerate until well chilled. (*Can be prepared up to 1 day ahead.*)

Release pan sides from charlotte. Place plate over charlotte. Invert onto plate. Remove pan bottom. Garnish with additional berries. Cut into wedges. Serve charlotte with raspberry sauce.

White Chocolate Crème Brûlée

4 servings

5 **large egg yolks**
½ **cup sugar**
2 **cups whipping cream**

3 **ounces imported white chocolate (such as Lindt), finely chopped**
¼ **teaspoon vanilla extract**

2 **tablespoons sugar**

Position rack in center of oven and preheat to 300°F. Whisk egg yolks and ¼ cup sugar in medium bowl. Bring cream and remaining ¼ cup sugar to simmer in heavy medium saucepan. Reduce heat to low. Gradually add chopped chocolate to cream mixture and whisk until smooth. Gradually whisk hot chocolate mixture into yolk mixture. Mix in vanilla.

Ladle custard into four 10-ounce custard cups. Place cups in large baking pan. Add enough hot water to pan to come halfway up sides of cups. Bake until custards are set in center, about 1 hour. Remove custards from water and cool. Cover custards and refrigerate overnight.

Preheat broiler. Sprinkle ½ tablespoon sugar over each custard. Broil until sugar caramelizes, watching carefully, about 2 minutes. Serve hot, or refrigerate custards up to 1 hour and serve cold.

Classic Chocolate Soufflés

8 servings

Sugar
½ **cup milk (do not use lowfat or nonfat)**
1¼ **cups sugar**
7 **ounces unsweetened chocolate, chopped**

6 **large egg whites**
4 **large egg yolks**
Powdered sugar

Preheat oven to 350°F. Butter eight ⅔-cup soufflé dishes. Sprinkle with sugar; tap out excess. Bring milk and 1 cup sugar to simmer in heavy large saucepan, stirring occasionally until sugar dissolves. Reduce heat to low. Add chocolate and stir until smooth. Pour into large bowl; let cool 10 minutes.

Using electric mixer, beat whites in another large bowl to soft peaks. Gradually add remaining ¼ cup sugar and beat until stiff but not dry. Whisk yolks into chocolate mixture. Whisk ¼ of whites into chocolate mixture to lighten. Fold in remaining whites. Divide mixture among prepared dishes. Bake until soufflés puff, about 16 minutes. Sift powdered sugar over soufflés.

❦ Frozen Desserts

Ice Cream with Marsala and Currants

2 servings

¼ cup dried currants
¼ cup orange juice
¼ cup Marsala
2 tablespoons sugar
½ cinnamon stick

½ teaspoon grated orange peel

Vanilla ice cream
Amaretti or other cookies, crumbled

Combine first 6 ingredients in heavy small saucepan. Boil until syrupy, stirring frequently, about 10 minutes. Cool slightly. Discard cinnamon.

Scoop ice cream into bowls. Spoon warm currant mixture over ice cream. Sprinkle with crumbled cookies and serve.

Coffee-Molasses Ice Cream with Molasses-glazed Pecans

6 servings

Ice Cream
3 cups whipping cream
1 cup milk (do not use lowfat or nonfat)
6 egg yolks
¾ cup light unsulfured molasses
¼ cup sugar
2 tablespoons instant coffee granules

Pecans
¼ cup light unsulfured molasses
¼ cup sugar
Pinch of salt
2 cups (about 8 ounces) pecan halves

For ice cream: Bring 2 cups cream and milk to boil in heavy medium saucepan. Remove from heat. Whisk egg yolks, molasses and sugar to blend in large bowl. Gradually whisk in hot cream mixture. Return mixture to saucepan and stir over medium-low heat until mixture thickens and leaves path on back of spoon when finger is drawn across, about 12 minutes; *do not boil or mixture will curdle.* Remove from heat. Mix in coffee granules and remaining 1 cup cream. Refrigerate coffee custard until well chilled. (*Can be prepared 2 days ahead.*)

Process coffee custard in ice cream maker according to the manufacturer's instructions. Freeze custard mixture until firm. (*Can be made 1 week ahead.*)

For pecans: Position rack in center of oven and preheat to 350°F. Butter large cookie sheet. Line another large cookie sheet with waxed paper. Combine molasses, sugar and salt in heavy medium saucepan. Boil 1 minute. Remove from heat. Add pecans and stir to coat well. Spread pecans on buttered cookie sheet. Bake until pecans are just beginning to brown, about 10 minutes. Immediately transfer pecans to waxed paper-lined cookie sheet and separate with 2 forks. Cool completely. (*Molasses-glazed pecans can be prepared 1 week ahead. Store at room temperature in airtight container.*)

Scoop ice cream into dishes. Top with pecans and serve immediately.

David Bishop

Chicken Soup with Wild Mushrooms and Herbed Matzo Balls and Beef Brisket Braised with Dried Fruit, Yams and Carrots

Garlic and Rosemary Steak with Potato-Onion Cakes

Island Chicken with Ginger-Lime Sauce

Lemon-Lime Tart with Fresh Raspberry Sauce

Chocolate Date-Nut Baklava and
Lemon-Lattice White Chocolate Cake

Myron Beck

Walnut and Coffee Tart with Coffee Cream

David Bishop

Toffee Cheesecake with Caramel Sauce

Raspberry and Coffee Tiramisù

David Bishop

Parfait aux Framboises

This luscious frozen dessert can be made without an ice cream maker. Begin preparing the recipe one day ahead.

10 servings

3/4 cup sugar
6 egg yolks
1/4 cup whipping cream
1 tablespoon vanilla
1 tablespoon Cognac or brandy

1 1/2 cups chilled whipping cream

1/2 cup sour cream
8 purchased macaroon cookies, crumbled

Fresh raspberries (optional)
Raspberry Sauce (see recipe)

Half fill medium saucepan with water and bring to boil. Whisk sugar, yolks and 1/4 cup cream in small metal bowl. Set bowl over saucepan of boiling water and whisk until candy thermometer registers 160°F, scraping down sides of bowl with rubber spatula, about 4 minutes. Remove from over water. Pour yolk mixture into large bowl. Using electric mixer, beat mixture until cool and thick, about 4 minutes. Beat in vanilla and brandy.

Beat 1 1/2 cups cream with sour cream to stiff peaks in medium bowl. Fold cream into yolk mixture in 2 batches. Gently fold in half of cookie crumbs. Pour mixture into 9-inch-diameter springform pan with 2-inch-high sides. Sprinkle with remaining crumbs. Freeze overnight.

Release sides of springform pan. Garnish dessert with fresh raspberries if desired. Slice into wedges and serve with raspberry sauce.

Raspberry Sauce

A perfect finish for the parfait, it's also great as a topping for fresh fruit.

Makes about 1 cup

1 10-ounce package frozen raspberries in syrup, thawed

Puree raspberries and syrup in blender or processor until smooth. Strain to remove seeds. (*Can be prepared 1 week ahead. Cover and refrigerate.*)

Lemon and Vanilla Bean Ice Cream

Makes about 4 cups

2 cups half and half
2/3 cup sugar
1 vanilla bean, split lengthwise

4 large egg yolks

1/4 cup fresh lemon juice
Pinch of salt

Combine half and half, 1/3 cup sugar and vanilla bean in heavy medium saucepan. Scald over medium heat. Scrape in vanilla bean seeds; discard bean. Whisk yolks with remaining 1/3 cup sugar in medium bowl until doubled in volume. Gradually whisk half and half mixture into yolk mixture. Return mixture to saucepan and stir over medium heat until custard thickens and leaves path on back of spoon when finger is drawn across, about 3 minutes; do not boil. Transfer custard to large bowl and refrigerate.

Stir lemon juice and salt into custard. Transfer to ice cream maker and process according to manufacturer's instructions. Place ice cream in container, cover and freeze. (*Can be prepared up to 2 days ahead.*) Let ice cream soften slightly at room temperature before serving.

Frozen Boysenberry and White Chocolate Parfait

Begin preparing this delicious frozen dessert at least one day ahead.

6 servings

Parfait
- 1 16-ounce bag frozen boysenberries or blackberries, thawed
- ¼ cup sugar
- 1 tablespoons crème de cassis or other berry-flavored liqueur
- ½ teaspoon fresh lemon juice

- ¾ cup sugar
- ¼ cup water
- 6 large egg yolks
- 3 ounces imported white chocolate (such as Lindt), chopped, melted

- 2 teaspoons vanilla extract
- 1⅔ cups chilled whipping cream

Sauce
- 1 16-ounce bag frozen boysenberries or blackberries, thawed
- ¼ cup sugar
- 2 tablespoons crème de cassis or other berry-flavored liqueur

Fresh boysenberries, blackberries or strawberries
Fresh mint sprigs

For parfait: Line 9 × 5-inch loaf pan with plastic wrap. Puree berries and ¼ cup sugar in blender until just smooth. Strain. Measure 1⅓ cups puree and place in heavy small saucepan. (Reserve any remaining puree for sauce.) Simmer 1⅓ cups puree over medium heat until reduced to scant 1 cup, stirring occasionally, about 8 minutes. Transfer to bowl and chill 30 minutes. Stir in cassis and lemon juice. Refrigerate reduced puree until ready to use.

Combine ¾ cup sugar, water and yolks in medium metal bowl. Set bowl over saucepan of simmering water. Using hand-held electric mixer, beat yolk mixture until it registers 140°F on candy thermometer, occasionally scraping down sides of bowl, about 5 minutes. Continue cooking 3 minutes, beating constantly. Remove from over water. Add warm melted chocolate and vanilla and beat until cool. Beat cream in another bowl to stiff peaks. Gently mix ¼ of whipped cream into chocolate mixture. Fold in remaining whipped cream.

Transfer 1⅓ cups chocolate mixture to medium bowl. Fold in reduced berry puree. Fill prepared loaf pan with ⅓ of remaining chocolate mixture. Cover with berry-chocolate mixture. Top with remaining chocolate mixture. Smooth top. Freeze parfait overnight (*Can be prepared 2 days ahead.*)

For sauce: Puree frozen boysenberries, sugar and crème de cassis in blender or processor until smooth. Strain. Add any berry puree reserved from parfait.

Unmold frozen parfait. Peel off plastic wrap. Slice into ½-inch-thick slices. Drizzle with sauce. Garnish with berries and fresh mint sprigs.

White Chocolate Ice Cream

Makes about 3 cups

- 1 cup milk (do not use lowfat or nonfat)
- 1 cup whipping cream
- ⅓ cup sugar

- 7 large egg yolks
- 7 ounces imported white chocolate (such as Lindt), chopped

Bring milk, cream and sugar to simmer in heavy large saucepan, stirring frequently. Whisk yolks in medium bowl to blend. Gradually whisk hot milk

mixture into yolks. Return mixture to saucepan and stir over medium-low heat until custard thickens and leaves path on back of spoon when finger is drawn across, about 4 minutes; do not boil. Remove pan from heat. Add chocolate and stir until melted and smooth. Strain into bowl. Refrigerate until cold. Transfer custard to ice cream maker and freeze according to manufacturer's instructions. Transfer to container and freeze. (*Can be prepared 1 week ahead; keep frozen.*)

Chocolate Brownie Sundaes

8 servings

1¾ cups all purpose flour
1 teaspoon baking powder
Pinch of salt
4 ounces unsweetened chocolate, chopped
1 cup vegetable oil
1 tablespoon instant espresso powder or instant coffee granules

2 teaspoons vanilla extract
4 large eggs
2 cups sugar

Purchased or homemade fudge sauce
2 pints ice cream

Preheat oven to 350°F. Butter 8-inch square baking pan with 2-inch-high sides. Sift flour, baking powder and salt into small bowl. Melt chocolate in heavy small saucepan over low heat, stirring until smooth. Pour into large bowl. Add oil, espresso powder and vanilla and whisk to blend. Whisk in eggs and sugar. Stir in dry ingredients. Pour batter into prepared pan. Bake until top is dry and toothpick inserted in center comes out with moist crumbs still attached, about 30 minutes. Immediately transfer to refrigerator. Refrigerate until cold, at least 3 hours. (*Can be prepared 1 day ahead. Store in refrigerator.*)

Heat fudge sauce if desired. Cut brownies into squares. Top with scoops of ice cream. Spoon sauce over and serve.

Peach Sundaes with Bourbon-Pecan Sauce

4 servings

1 tablespoon fresh lemon juice
3 large firm ripe peaches (about 1¼ pounds)
6 tablespoons (¾ stick) unsalted butter
½ cup firmly packed golden brown sugar

3 tablespoons whipping cream
½ cup toasted pecan pieces
1 tablespoon bourbon

1 pint vanilla ice cream

Place lemon juice in medium bowl. Peel and pit peaches. Slice thinly into bowl; toss to coat with lemon juice. Melt butter in heavy medium saucepan over medium heat. Add brown sugar and stir until mixture thickens and bubbles. Add cream 1 tablespoon at a time and stir until sugar dissolves and sauce is thick and smooth, about 3 minutes. Stir in peaches, pecans and bourbon. Cook until sauce is heated through, stirring constantly, about 1 minute longer.

Scoop ice cream into bowls. Spoon sauce over and serve.

Brazilian Banana and White Chocolate Ice Cream Torte (Cover Recipe)

Giving a nod to tropical fruit, this irresistible treat combines rich ice cream with a nut crust and thick fudge sauce.

12 servings

Crust
- 3 cups walnuts (about 12 ounces)
- 1 cup whole almonds
- ⅓ cup firmly packed dark brown sugar
- ¼ cup (½ stick) unsalted butter, melted, cooled

Ice Cream
- 3 cups whipping cream
- 1 cup half and half
- ¾ cup sugar
- 4 large egg yolks
- 8 ounces imported white chocolate (such as Lindt), chopped

- 1½ pounds very ripe bananas
- 3 tablespoons fresh lemon juice

Sauce
- ¾ cup whipping cream
- ¼ cup light corn syrup
- 8 ounces bittersweet (not unsweetened) or semisweet chocolate, chopped

- 3 large ripe bananas, peeled, cut on diagonal into ¼-inch-wide slices
- 15 (about) small strawberries with stems

For crust: Preheat oven to 350°F. Finely chop all nuts with sugar in processor. Add butter and blend until well combined. Press mixture firmly onto sides, then bottom of 9-inch-diameter springform pan with 2¾-inch-high sides. Place crust in freezer 10 minutes. Bake crust until light brown, about 20 minutes. Transfer to rack; cool crust completely.

For ice cream: Bring 1 cup cream, half and half and sugar to simmer in heavy medium saucepan, stirring occasionally. Whisk yolks in medium bowl. Whisk in hot cream mixture. Return mixture to saucepan and stir over medium-low heat until custard thickens and leaves path on back of spoon when finger is drawn across, about 5 minutes; do not boil. Strain into large bowl. Add white chocolate; whisk until white chocolate is melted. Mix in remaining 2 cups cream. Refrigerate custard until cold.

Peel and slice 1½ pounds bananas. Puree bananas with lemon juice in processor. Mix puree into custard. Transfer custard to ice cream maker and process according to manufacturer's instructions. Spoon ice cream into crust; smooth top. Cover and freeze overnight. (*Can be prepared 1 week ahead; keep frozen.*)

For sauce: Bring cream and syrup to simmer in heavy medium saucepan. Reduce heat to low. Add chocolate; whisk until smooth. Cool to lukewarm. (*Can be prepared 1 day ahead. Cover and refrigerate. Rewarm sauce over low heat before using; do not boil.*)

Remove pan sides from torte. Arrange bananas and strawberries in alternating diagonal rows atop ice cream. Cut into wedges. Serve with sauce.

Mango-Macadamia Nut Ice Cream

Be sure to use extra-ripe mangoes when preparing this rich, creamy dessert.

Makes about 5 cups

- 2 cups whipping cream
- 1 cup milk (do not use lowfat or nonfat)
- 6 egg yolks
- 1 cup sugar

- 2 large ripe mangoes (about 22 ounces), peeled, pitted, diced
- 2 teaspoons fresh lime juice
- ½ teaspoon grated lime peel
- 1 cup unsalted macadamia nuts, toasted, coarsely chopped

Bring 2 cups whipping cream and 1 cup milk to boil in heavy large saucepan. Whisk yolks and sugar to blend in medium bowl. Gradually whisk hot cream

into yolk mixture. Return to same saucepan. Stir over low heat until custard thickens and leaves path on back of spoon when finger is drawn across, about 5 minutes. Immediately transfer custard to blender. Add mangoes and blend until smooth. Chill custard. Stir in remaining ingredients. Process in ice cream maker according to manufacturer's instructions. Freeze ice cream in covered container. (*Can be prepared 2 days ahead.*)

❦ *Pies, Tarts and Pastries*

Walnut and Coffee Tart with Coffee Cream

8 servings

Crust
- 1 cup unbleached all purpose flour
- 1 tablespoon dark brown sugar
- ¼ teaspoon salt
- 6 tablespoons (¾ stick) chilled unsalted butter, cut into small pieces
- 1 large egg yolk
- 1 tablespoon ice water

Filling
- 1¼ cups chopped walnuts (about 5 ounces)
- 2 tablespoons instant coffee granules
- 2 tablespoons water
- ½ cup firmly packed dark brown sugar
- 3 large eggs
- ½ cup light corn syrup
- ¼ cup (½ stick) unsalted butter, melted, cooled
- ⅛ teaspoon salt

Coffee Cream
- 1 teaspoon instant coffee granules
- 1 teaspoon water
- 1 cup chilled whipping cream
- 2 tablespoons powdered sugar

For crust: Combine flour, brown sugar and salt in medium bowl. Add butter and cut in with fingers or pastry blender until mixture resembles coarse meal. Beat egg yolk and water in small bowl to blend. Pour over flour mixture. Stir with fork until mixture forms dough. Gather into ball; flatten into disk. Wrap dough and chill until firm, at least 30 minutes.

Preheat oven to 400°F. Roll dough out on lightly floured surface to 12-inch-diameter round. Roll up on rolling pin and transfer to 9-inch-diameter tart pan with removable bottom. Fit dough into pan and trim edges. Freeze until firm, about 20 minutes. Bake crust until golden brown, piercing with toothpick if crust bubbles, about 15 minutes. Cool slightly. Maintain oven temperature.

For filling: Place walnuts on cookie sheet and toast in oven until just golden brown and fragrant, about 8 minutes. Cool. Reduce oven temperature to 350°F.

Dissolve coffee granules in 2 tablespoons water in large bowl. Add brown sugar and whisk until smooth. Whisk in eggs, corn syrup, butter and salt. Stir in walnuts. Pour filling into prepared crust and bake until set, about 30 minutes. Cool tart on rack. (*Tart can be prepared 6 hours ahead. Cover tart loosely and let stand at room temperature.*)

For cream: Dissolve coffee granules in 1 teaspoon water in small bowl. Whip cream and sugar until medium-soft peaks form. Add coffee mixture and continue beating until stiff peaks form. Serve tart with whipped cream.

Black Bottom Banana Cream Pie

8 servings

1 **Buttermilk Pie Crust Dough disk (see recipe)**

Ganache

4 **ounces bittersweet (not unsweetened) or semisweet chocolate, chopped**
¼ **cup whipping cream**
2 **tablespoons (¼ stick) unsalted butter**

2 **large firm ripe bananas (about 1¼ pounds), cut into ⅔-inch-thick slices**

Filling

1½ **teaspoons vanilla extract**
1½ **teaspoons dark rum**
½ **teaspoon unflavored gelatin**
½ **cup whipping cream**
5 **large egg yolks**
3 **tablespoons sugar**

½ **cup chilled whipping cream**

Topping

¾ **cup chilled whipping cream**
2 **tablespoons sugar**
2 **firm ripe bananas, thinly sliced on diagonal**

Position rack in lowest third of oven and preheat to 400°F. Roll out pie crust disk on lightly floured surface to 13-inch-diameter round (about ⅛ inch thick). Roll up dough on rolling pin and transfer to 9-inch-diameter glass pie plate. Trim edges of crust, leaving ½-inch overhang. Fold excess dough under. Crimp edges. Freeze until crust is firm, about 15 minutes.

Line pie crust with foil. Fill foil with dried beans or pie weights. Bake until crust is set, about 15 minutes. Remove beans and foil and continue baking until crust is golden brown, piercing with toothpick if crust bubbles, about 12 minutes. Cool pie crust completely.

For ganache: Stir chocolate, cream and butter in heavy small saucepan over low heat until chocolate and butter melt and mixture is smooth. Spoon 6 tablespoons ganache into crust. Spread with back of spoon to cover bottom completely. Let stand until ganache is cool but not set, about 20 minutes. Reserve remaining ganache in saucepan.

Arrange banana slices atop ganache, pressing bananas lightly into ganache.

For filling: Combine vanilla and rum in small bowl. Sprinkle gelatin over. Let stand 10 minutes to soften gelatin. Bring ½ cup cream to simmer in heavy small saucepan. Whisk egg yolks and sugar to blend in another small bowl. Gradually whisk in hot cream. Return mixture to saucepan. Stir over medium-low heat until mixture thickens and leaves path on back of spoon when finger is drawn across, about 4 minutes; do not boil. Add gelatin and stir until gelatin melts. Transfer custard to large bowl. Chill until cool but not set, stirring occasionally, approximately 20 minutes.

Whip ½ cup chilled cream to medium peaks in medium bowl. Fold into custard in 2 additions. Spoon custard into crust. Chill until set, about 2 hours.

Stir reserved ganache over low heat until just warm and pourable. Carefully pour ganache onto center of filling. Tilt pie, rotating to spread ganache to within ¼ inch of pie edge. Chill until ganache is set, about 15 minutes. (*Can be prepared 8 hours ahead; keep refrigerated.*)

For topping: Beat ¾ cup whipping cream and 2 tablespoons sugar to firm peaks. Spoon whipped cream into pastry bag fitted with large star tip. Pipe rosettes around inside edge of crust. Place banana slices in ring alongside rosettes. Cut pie into wedges and serve.

Orange-Rhubarb Pie with Apricots

8 servings

1¾ cups sugar
1 2-inch piece vanilla bean, quartered
½ orange (unpeeled), cut into chunks
1 20-ounce bag frozen rhubarb
½ cup cranberries, coarsely chopped

½ cup thinly sliced dried apricots
¼ cup all purpose flour

2 Buttermilk Pie Crust Dough disks (see recipe)
Sour Cream Topping (see recipe)

Position rack in lowest third of oven and preheat to 400°F. Combine sugar and vanilla bean in processor and blend until vanilla bean is finely chopped. Add orange and process until orange is finely chopped. Transfer mixture to large bowl. Add rhubarb, cranberries, apricots and flour and toss well.

Roll out 1 pie crust disk on lightly floured surface to 13-inch round (about ⅛ inch thick). Roll up dough on rolling pin and transfer to 9-inch-diameter pie plate. Gently press into place. Trim edges of crust, leaving ¾-inch overhang. Roll out second disk on lightly floured surface to 13-inch round. Cut round into ½-inch-wide strips. Spoon rhubarb mixture into crust. Place strips atop pie, forming lattice. Pinch edges to seal strips to crust edge. Fold overhang under strip ends so that crust is flush with edge of pie pan. Crimp edges to make decorative border. Bake until crust is golden and filling bubbles around edges, covering edges of crust if browning too quickly, about 55 minutes. Cool. Serve pie warm or at room temperature with Sour Cream Topping.

Sour Cream Topping

Makes about 1 cup

1 cup sour cream
2 tablespoons firmly packed dark brown sugar

½ teaspoon grated orange peel

Combine all ingredients in small bowl. (*Can be prepared 2 days ahead. Cover tightly with plastic and refrigerate.*)

Three-Nut Pie with Cranberries

Tart cranberries provide delicious contrast to the rich nut filling.

8 servings

1 Buttermilk Pie Crust Dough disk (see recipe)

½ cup coarsely chopped walnuts
½ cup coarsely chopped pecans
½ cup sliced almonds

¾ cup firmly packed dark brown sugar
½ cup light corn syrup

¼ cup plus 2 tablespoons (¾ stick) unsalted butter, melted, room temperature
3 large eggs
2 tablespoons unsulfured molasses (light)
1 teaspoon vanilla extract
¼ teaspoon salt
1½ cups cranberries (about 6 ounces)

Preheat oven to 400°F. Roll out pie crust disk on lightly floured surface to 13-inch round (about ⅛ inch thick). Roll up dough on rolling pin and transfer to 9-inch-diameter glass pie plate. Gently press into place. Trim edges of crust, leaving ¾-inch overhang. Fold overhang under crust so that crust is flush with

edge of pie pan. Crimp edges of crust to make decorative border. Freeze crust until firm, about 15 minutes.

Line pie crust with foil, leaving 3-inch overhang. Fill foil with dried beans or pie weights. Fold extra foil gently over crust edges. Bake until crust is set, about 15 minutes. Remove foil and beans and continue baking until crust just begins to color, piercing with toothpick if crust bubbles, about 10 minutes. Cool completely. Maintain oven temperature.

Meanwhile, combine nuts on cookie sheet. Toast until just golden, about 10 minutes. Cool completely.

Whisk brown sugar and next 6 ingredients to blend to bowl. Stir in nuts and cranberries. Pour filling into prepared crust. Bake until center of filling is set, about 45 minutes. Cool completely.

Gingered Pear Pie with Golden Raisins

8 servings

¾ cup golden raisins
¼ cup plus 2 tablespoons minced crystallized ginger (about 2½ ounces)

3 pounds ripe medium pears (about 7), peeled, cored, sliced ½ inch thick
½ cup sugar
3 tablespoons butter, melted
2 tablespoons quick-cooking tapioca

1 tablespoon fresh lemon juice
1¼ teaspoons ground cinnamon
¼ teaspoon ground nutmeg
2 Buttermilk Pie Crust Dough disks (see recipe)

1 egg
2 tablespoons milk

Vanilla ice cream

Combine raisins and ginger in heavy small saucepan. Add enough water to just cover. Simmer over low heat until liquid is absorbed, about 15 minutes. Cool.

Position rack in lowest third of oven and preheat to 400°F. Combine pears and next 6 ingredients in large bowl. Stir in raisin mixture. Roll out 1 pie crust disk on lightly floured surface to 13-inch round (about ⅛ inch thick). Roll up dough on rolling pin and transfer to 9-inch-diameter glass pie plate. Gently press into place. Trim edges of crust, leaving ¼-inch overhang. Spoon pear mixture into crust-lined pan, mounding in center.

Roll out second crust disk on lightly floured surface to 13-inch-diameter round. Roll up on rolling pin and unroll over pie. Trim edges, leaving ¾-inch overhang. Fold overhang of top crust under edge of bottom crust. Pinch edges together to seal. Crimp edges to make decorative border. Gather and reroll scraps. Cut out decorative shapes. Beat egg with milk in small bowl for glaze. Brush top of pie with glaze. Arrange dough cutouts decoratively atop pie. Brush cutouts with glaze. Make several slashes in top crust so steam can escape.

Bake pie until crust is golden brown and juices bubble up through slashes, covering crust edges with foil if browning too quickly, about 1 hour. Cool slightly. Serve warm with vanilla ice cream.

Buttermilk Pie Crust Dough

Makes enough for 2 crusts

2½ cups unbleached all purpose flour
2 tablespoons sugar
1 teaspoon salt
½ cup (1 stick) chilled unsalted butter, diced

½ cup chilled solid vegetable shortening
¼ cup plus 2 tablespoons buttermilk

Combine flour, sugar and salt in large bowl. Add butter and shortening. Cut in using hands or pastry blender until mixture resembles coarse meal. Add buttermilk and stir with fork until moist clumps form. (Dough can also be prepared in processor. Using on/off turns, cut butter and shortening into dry ingredients until coarse meal forms. Add buttermilk and process just until moist clumps form.) Press together to form dough. Divide dough in half. Gather dough into balls; flatten into disks. Wrap separately and chill 1 hour. (*Can be prepared ahead. Refrigerate 1 week or freeze 1 month. Let dough stand at room temperature to soften slightly before using.*)

Caramelized Apple Tart

Serve this homey dessert with vanilla ice cream or whipped cream.

10 servings

Pastry
1¾ cups plus 2 tablespoons all purpose flour
1½ tablespoons sugar
½ teaspoon salt
6 tablespoons chilled solid vegetable shortening
6 tablespoons (¾ stick) chilled unsalted butter, cut into pieces
7 tablespoons (about) cold water

Filling
1 cup sugar
⅓ cup fresh lemon juice

¼ cup water
1¼ teaspoons ground cinnamon
¾ teaspoon grated lemon peel
½ teaspoon ground nutmeg
⅛ teaspoon ground cloves
4 pounds tart green apples (about 10 medium)

6 tablespoons (¾ stick) unsalted butter

Vanilla ice cream or whipped cream (optional)

For pastry: Combine flour, sugar and salt in processor. Add shortening and butter and cut in using on/off turns until mixture resembles coarse meal. Using on/off turns, blend in enough water 1 tablespoon at a time to form dough that just holds together. Gather dough into ball; flatten into disk. Wrap in plastic and refrigerate 30 minutes. (*Can be prepared 1 day ahead. Soften dough slightly at room temperature before rolling.*)

Lightly spray 10-inch-diameter tart pan with 2-inch-high sides with non-stick vegetable oil spray. Roll dough out between sheets of plastic wrap to ⅛-inch-thick round. Peel off top sheet of plastic. Invert dough into prepared pan. Press dough onto bottom and up sides of pan. Peel off plastic. Trim edges. Refrigerate crust for 30 minutes.

Preheat oven to 375°F. Line tart crust with foil. Fill with dried beans or pie weights. Bake 15 minutes. Remove foil and beans. Pierce bottom of crust with fork. Bake crust until golden brown, about 20 minutes. Cool.

For filling: Mix first 7 ingredients in large bowl. Peel, core and quarter apples and add to sugar mixture. Let stand 45 minutes, stirring occasionally.

Preheat oven to 375°F. Melt 3 tablespoons butter in each of 2 heavy large skillets over medium-low heat. Add half of apples and their juices to each skillet and bring to simmer. Cover and cook 8 minutes. Increase heat to medium. Uncover and cook until sugar caramelizes and apples are tender, turning apples occasionally, about 12 minutes.

Arrange apples on their sides in tart crust, overlapping slightly. Spoon caramelized juices over. Bake 20 minutes. Cool slightly. (*Can be prepared 6 hours ahead. Let stand at room temperature.*) Serve warm or at room temperature with vanilla ice cream or whipped cream.

Lemon-Lime Tart with Fresh Raspberry Sauce

8 servings

Crust
- 1½ cups cake flour
- ½ cup (1 stick) unsalted butter, room temperature
- 5 tablespoons sugar
- 1 large egg yolk
- 1 teaspoon finely chopped lemon peel (yellow part only)
- ½ vanilla bean, split lengthwise

Filling
- 5 large eggs
- 1 large egg yolk
- 1 cup sugar
- ⅔ cup whipping cream
- 2½ tablespoons fresh lemon juice
- 2 tablespoons fresh lime juice
- 1½ tablespoons finely chopped lemon peel (yellow part only)
- 1 teaspoon finely chopped lime peel (green part only)

Sauce
- 2 ½-pint baskets raspberries or 1 1-pint basket strawberries
- 1 tablespoon sugar

Powdered sugar

For crust: Mound flour on work surface. Make well in center. Combine butter, sugar, yolk and lemon peel in center of well. Scrape in seeds from vanilla bean. Gradually incorporate flour into butter mixture, blending until coarse meal forms. Knead until just smooth. Flatten into disk. Wrap dough in plastic and refrigerate until firm, about 1 hour.

Preheat oven to 325°F. Grease and lightly flour 10-inch-diameter tart pan with removable bottom. Roll dough out on lightly floured surface to 12-inch round. Transfer dough to prepared pan; crimp and finish edges. Refrigerate crust for 15 minutes.

Line crust with parchment or foil. Fill with dried beans or pie weights. Bake until crust is set, about 15 minutes. Remove beans and parchment. Bake crust until golden brown, about 25 minutes more. Cool on rack. Maintain oven temperature. (*Can be prepared 1 day ahead. Cover; store at room temperature.*)

For filling: Whisk eggs, yolk and sugar together in medium bowl. Gradually mix in cream, lemon and lime juices and chopped peels. Pour filling into crust. Bake until filling is set, about 40 minutes. Cool to room temperature on rack.

For sauce: Puree one ½-pint basket of raspberries or half of strawberries with sugar in blender. Strain sauce.

Dust tart with powdered sugar. Garnish with berries and serve with sauce.

Chocolate Date-Nut Baklava

Makes 24 pieces

Syrup
- 1 cup sugar
- ½ cup water
  Pinch of ground allspice
  Pinch of ground ginger
  Pinch of ground cloves

Filling
- 8 ounces (about 2 cups) walnuts
- 6 ounces bittersweet (not unsweetened) or semisweet chocolate, cut into ½-inch pieces
- 6 ounces (about 1 cup) whole pitted dates
- 2 tablespoons sugar

- 1 tablespoon ground cinnamon
- 1 egg, beaten to blend

- 11 sheets frozen phyllo pastry (about ½ pound), thawed
- ¾ cup (1½ sticks) unsalted butter, melted

- 2 ounces bittersweet (not unsweetened) or semisweet chocolate, chopped
- 1 tablespoon unsalted butter
- 24 walnut halves
  Whipped cream (optional)

For syrup: Bring all ingredients to boil in heavy small saucepan, stirring until sugar dissolves. Continue boiling 1 minute. Cool completely. (*Can be prepared up to 2 days ahead. Cover and store at room temperature.*)

For filling: Combine 8 ounces walnuts, 6 ounces chocolate, dates, sugar and cinnamon in processor. Coarsely chop using on/off turns. Transfer filling to medium bowl. Mix in beaten egg.

Position rack in center of oven and preheat to 350°F. Lightly butter 13 × 9 × 2-inch metal baking pan. Place 1 phyllo sheet on work surface (keep remainder covered with plastic and damp towel to prevent drying). Brush phyllo with butter. Top with second phyllo sheet and brush with butter. Arrange sheets buttered side up and lengthwise in prepared pan, covering bottom and ends of pan. Brush another phyllo sheet with butter. Fold phyllo in half forming 8 × 12-inch rectangle and brush with butter. Repeat with 2 more phyllo sheets. Place 3 folded phyllo sheets in bottom of pan, buttered side up. Sprinkle half of filling over. Butter another phyllo sheet and fold in half. Butter top and place atop filling. Sprinkle remaining filling over. Repeat buttering and folding with 3 more phyllo sheets. Place atop filling. Butter last 2 phyllo sheets. Place lengthwise in pan, tucking in sides and ends of top and bottom sheets to enclose filling.

Carefully cut through top layers of phyllo (do not cut through to filling) to form twenty-four 2-inch squares. Pour any remaining butter over. Bake until top is golden brown, about 45 minutes. Immediately spoon syrup over baklava. Cool completely. Cover and let stand at room temperature overnight.

Melt 2 ounces chocolate and 1 tablespoon butter in heavy small saucepan. Dip walnut halves halfway into chocolate; shake off excess. Place on waxed paper and refrigerate until chocolate is set, about 30 minutes. (*Can be prepared 1 day ahead. Cover walnuts with waxed paper.*) Cut baklava into squares on score lines. Transfer baklava squares to platter. Place chocolate-dipped walnut half atop each square. Serve with whipped cream if desired.

Caramel-Pecan Black Bottom Pie

*Two new flavors enhance
a sweet classic.*

8 servings

Crust
1⅓ cups sifted all purpose flour
  3 tablespoons sugar
 ¼ teaspoon salt
  7 tablespoons cold unsalted butter,
     cut into ½-inch pieces
  2 tablespoons ice water
  1 large egg yolk
 ½ teaspoon vanilla extract

Filling
  2 tablespoons brandy
 ½ teaspoon vanilla extract
  1 teaspoon unflavored gelatin
  5 ounces bittersweet (not
     unsweetened) or semisweet
     chocolate, finely chopped

 ½ cup sugar
  3 tablespoons cornstarch
 ¼ teaspoon salt
  2 cups half and half
  4 large egg yolks

Topping
⅔ cup sugar
⅓ cup water
½ cup plus 1 tablespoon whipping
   cream
¼ cup (½ stick) unsalted butter
 1 cup toasted pecans, chopped

For crust: Combine flour, sugar and salt in processor. Add butter and blend using on/off turns until mixture resembles coarse meal. Beat water, egg yolk and vanilla together in small bowl. Add egg mixture to processor and process until large moist clumps form. Gather dough into ball; flatten into disk. Wrap in plastic and refrigerate 30 minutes. (*Dough can be prepared up to 2 days ahead. Let dough stand at room temperature to soften slightly before continuing.*)

Position rack in center of oven and preheat to 350°F. Lightly butter 9-inch-diameter pie pan. Roll dough out on floured surface to 13-inch round. Transfer to prepared pan. Fold edges under and crimp to form high fluted edge. Freeze until firm, about 15 minutes. Line crust with foil and fill with dried beans or pie weights. Bake until sides are set, about 20 minutes. Remove foil and beans. Pierce bottom of crust in several places with fork and bake crust until golden brown, about 20 minutes. Cool on rack.

For filling: Combine brandy and vanilla in small bowl. Sprinkle gelatin over and let stand 10 minutes. Place chocolate in medium bowl. Mix sugar, cornstarch and salt in heavy medium saucepan. Gradually whisk half and half and egg yolks into sugar mixture. Cook over medium-high heat until custard is thick and smooth and begins to boil, whisking constantly, about 3 minutes. Quickly add 1¼ cups custard to chocolate. Stir until chocolate melts and mixture is smooth. Add brandy and gelatin mixture to remaining hot custard. Stir until gelatin dissolves. Spread chocolate filling in crust. Spread brandy filling over. Refrigerate uncovered until pie is completely cool.

For topping: Heat sugar and water in heavy small saucepan over low heat, stirring until sugar dissolves. Increase heat and boil, without stirring, until mixture is deep amber, brushing down sugar crystals from sides of pan with wet pastry brush, about 11 minutes. Remove from heat and add cream (mixture will bubble up). Add butter and stir until smooth. Stir over low heat until color deepens and caramel thickens slightly, about 3 minutes. Mix in pecans. Transfer to bowl. Chill until cool but not set, stirring occasionally, about 30 minutes.

Spoon topping over brandy layer. Chill pie until topping is set, about 2 hours. (*Can be prepared 1 day ahead. Cover and refrigerate.*)

Coffee and Chocolate Paris-Brest with Warm Caramel Sauce

The espresso-flavored cream puff pastry and fluffy coffee and chocolate custard filling vary from the traditional plain pastry and praline buttercream. Delicious on its own, this is even better with the chocolate caramel sauce.

8 servings

Sauce
- ¾ cup sugar
- ¼ cup water
- ½ cup whipping cream
- 1 tablespoon unsalted butter
- ½ ounce bittersweet (not unsweetened) or semisweet chocolate, chopped
- ½ teaspoon instant espresso powder or instant coffee granules

Filling
- ½ cup sugar
- 4 large egg yolks
- ¼ cup unbleached all purpose flour
- 1½ cups half and half
- 4 teaspoons instant espresso powder or instant coffee granules
- ½ vanilla bean, split lengthwise

- 2 ounces bittersweet (not unsweetened) or semisweet chocolate, chopped
- ½ cup chilled whipping cream

Pastry
- ½ cup milk (do not use lowfat or nonfat)
- ¼ cup (½ stick) unsalted butter, cut into small pieces
- 2 tablespoons sugar
- 1½ teaspoons instant espresso powder or instant coffee granules
  Pinch of salt
- ½ cup unbleached all purpose flour
- 3 large eggs
- ⅓ cup sliced almonds

  Powdered sugar
- 2 tablespoons dark rum

For sauce: Stir sugar and water in heavy small saucepan over low heat until sugar dissolves. Increase heat and boil without stirring until syrup turns deep golden brown, occasionally washing down sides of pan with wet pastry brush, about 9 minutes. Add cream (mixture will bubble up). Reduce heat to very low. Stir until caramel dissolves completely and mixture is smooth. Add butter, chocolate and espresso powder and stir until smooth. (*Sauce can be prepared 2 days ahead. Cover tightly and refrigerate.*)

For filling: Whisk sugar and yolks in medium bowl until thick, about 1 minute. Add flour and beat until well blended. Combine half and half and espresso powder in heavy medium saucepan. Scrape in vanilla seeds; add pod. Bring just to simmer over medium heat. Gradually whisk hot half and half mixture into egg mixture. Return egg mixture to same saucepan and cook until mixture is very thick and boils, whisking constantly. Pour mixture into medium bowl. Remove vanilla pod. Add chocolate and whisk until smooth. Press plastic wrap directly on surface of filling to prevent skin from forming; cool.

Whisk filling until smooth. Beat chilled whipping cream in another medium bowl until stiff peaks form. Fold whipped cream into filling in 2 additions. Cover and chill at least 2 hours. (*Can be prepared 8 hours ahead.*)

For pastry: Position rack in center of oven and preheat to 425°F. Stack 2 cookie sheets. Line top cookie sheet with parchment. Trace 8½-inch-diameter circle on parchment, using cake pan as guide. Turn parchment over. Butter circle lightly and then dust with flour.

Combine milk, butter, sugar, espresso powder and salt in heavy medium saucepan. Bring just to boil over medium heat, stirring until butter melts and sugar dissolves. Add flour and cook 3 minutes, stirring vigorously with wooden spoon (mixture will form ball). Remove from heat. Make well in center of dough. Break 1 egg into well. Using wooden spoon, beat rapidly until egg is

incorporated and dough is smooth, about 1 minute. Repeat with second egg. Beat third egg to blend in small bowl. Reserve 1 tablespoon egg for glaze. Add remaining beaten egg to dough and beat until smooth.

Fit pastry bag with ¾-inch (no. 7) star tip. Transfer warm dough to bag. Pipe ¾-inch-wide ring over traced circle on parchment. Pipe second ring inside first, making certain batter adheres to inside of first ring. Pipe third ring atop center of first two rings. Brush lightly with egg glaze. Sprinkle with almonds.

Bake pastry 2 minutes. Reduce oven temperature to 375°F and bake until pastry is golden brown and firm to touch, about 40 minutes longer. Turn off heat. Leave pastry in oven 5 minutes. Remove from oven. Carefully remove pastry from parchment. Using serrated knife, cut pastry in half horizontally. Arrange cut sides up on rack (pastry will appear moist and slightly doughy inside). Cool pastry completely.

Fit clean pastry bag with ¾-inch (no. 7) star tip. Transfer filling to bag. Place pastry bottom on platter. Pipe filling into pastry in large circular mounds. Set top of pastry over filling. Dust lightly with powdered sugar. Gently heat sauce in heavy small saucepan. Mix in rum. Using serrated knife, cut pastry into wedges. Serve, passing sauce separately.

 Cakes

Toffee Cheesecake with Caramel Sauce

10 servings

Crust
- 1½ cups graham cracker crumbs
- 6 tablespoons (¾ stick) unsalted butter, melted
- ¼ cup firmly packed dark brown sugar

Filling
- 2 pounds cream cheese, room temperature
- 1½ cups sugar
- 5 large eggs, room temperature
- 2½ teaspoons vanilla extract
- 2 teaspoons fresh lemon juice

Topping
- 1¼ cups sugar
- ⅓ cup water
- 1 cup whipping cream
- ½ cup (1 stick) unsalted butter, cut into small pieces, room temperature
- 1 teaspoon vanilla extract

- ¾ cup whipping cream
- 2 tablespoons sugar
- 3 1.4-ounce toffee candy bars (such as Skor), broken into pieces

For crust: Preheat oven to 350°F. Lightly butter inside of 9-inch-diameter springform pan with 2¾-inch-high sides. Combine crumbs, butter and brown sugar in small bowl. Press crumbs over bottom and 1 inch up sides of pan. Chill.

For filling: Using electric mixer, beat cream cheese until fluffy. Add sugar and beat until smooth. Beat in eggs 1 at a time. Mix in vanilla and lemon juice.

Pour filling into prepared crust. Bake until cake rises about ½ inch over rim and center moves only slightly when pan is shaken, about 1 hour 15 minutes. Cool on rack. (Cake will fall as it cools, sinking in center.) Cover and refrigerate until well chilled, at least 6 hours. (*Can be made 1 day ahead.*)

For topping: Heat sugar and water in heavy medium saucepan over low heat, stirring until sugar dissolves. Increase heat and boil without stirring until mixture is rich caramel color, occasionally swirling and washing down sides of pan with brush dipped into cold water, about 8 minutes. Reduce heat to very low. Add cream (mixture will bubble up) and stir until smooth. Mix in butter. Cool slightly. Mix in vanilla extract.

Using small sharp knife, cut around sides of pan to loosen cake. Release pan sides. Pour ⅔ cup caramel sauce into center of cake. Cover remaining caramel sauce and let stand at room temperature. Chill cake until caramel topping is almost set, about 2 hours. (*Can be prepared 8 hours ahead.*)

Whip ¾ cup cream with 2 tablespoons sugar in medium bowl until firm peaks form. Spoon cream into pastry bag fitted with star tip. Pipe cream decoratively around edge of cake. Arrange toffee pieces in whipped cream border. Refrigerate cheesecake until serving.

Cut cake into wedges. Serve, passing remaining caramel sauce separately.

Chocolate, Cherry and Marsala Cassata

6 servings

Filling
⅓ cup dried currants
5 tablespoons Marsala
1 17-ounce can dark sweet pitted cherries in syrup, drained, syrup reserved for frosting

1 15-ounce container ricotta cheese
¼ cup sugar

2 tablespoons whipping cream
1 16-ounce pound cake

Chocolate Frosting
12 ounces semisweet chocolate, chopped
¼ cup Marsala
1 cup (2 sticks) chilled unsalted butter, cut into pieces

For filling: Combine dried currants and 2 tablespoons Marsala in small bowl. Let currants macerate 15 minutes. Cut cherries into eighths and drain on paper towels. Drain currants. Set aside.

Puree ricotta, sugar, remaining 3 tablespoons Marsala and cream in processor until smooth. Transfer to bowl. Gently mix in currants and cherries.

Peel any loose crust from pound cake and discard. Cut pound cake lengthwise into 3 horizontal layers. Place bottom layer on serving platter. Spread half of filling over. Place second pound cake layer atop filling. Spread remaining filling over. Arrange third pound cake layer atop filling. Smooth sides with rubber spatula. Refrigerate cassata until filling is firm, about 2 hours.

For frosting: Combine ½ cup reserved cherry syrup, semisweet chocolate and Marsala in heavy medium saucepan. Stir over low heat until chocolate melts and mixture is smooth. Remove from heat. Add unsalted butter a few pieces at a time and whisk until melted. Refrigerate frosting until thickened to spreading consistency, stirring occasionally, about 20 minutes.

Slide sheets of waxed paper under edges of cassata. Transfer 1 cup chocolate frosting to pastry bag fitted with medium star tip. Spread remaining chocolate frosting over sides and top of cassata. Pipe frosting in pastry bag in swirls on long sides and in rosettes along upper edges of cassata. Refrigerate until set. (*Can be prepared 1 day ahead; keep refrigerated.*) Let cassata stand at room temperature 20 minutes before serving.

German Lebkuchen Cake with White Chocolate Frosting (Cover Recipe)

This moist cake takes its cues from the flavors and spices found in the classic Lebkuchen cookie. It's brushed with an orange-scented honey syrup, frosted with a creamy white chocolate icing and then surrounded by almonds.

12 servings

Honey Syrup
2 to 3 large oranges
½ cup honey
⅔ cup orange juice

Cake
¾ cup (1½ sticks) unsalted butter, room temperature
¾ cup firmly packed golden brown sugar
1 tablespoon vanilla extract
1¼ teaspoons ground cinnamon
¾ teaspoon ground cloves
¾ teaspoon ground nutmeg
¾ teaspoon ground allspice
½ teaspoon salt
2 large eggs, room temperature

1¾ cups all purpose flour
1½ teaspoons baking soda
¾ teaspoon baking powder
⅔ cup half and half
1 tablespoon lemon juice
⅔ cup dried currants

Frosting
12 ounces imported white chocolate (such as Lindt), chopped
1 cup (2 sticks) unsalted butter, room temperature
12 ounces cream cheese, room temperature

3 cups toasted sliced almonds
Orange slices or orange peel ribbon

For syrup: Using vegetable peeler, remove peel (orange part only) from oranges in strips. Mince enough peel to measure 4 tablespoons. Mix honey, orange juice and 2 tablespoons orange peel (reserve remaining 2 tablespoons peel for cake) in heavy medium saucepan. Boil until reduced to ¾ cup, about 10 minutes.

For cake: Preheat oven to 350°F. Butter 9-inch square baking pan with 2-inch-high sides. Line bottom with waxed paper. Butter paper. Dust pan with flour. Using electric mixer, beat first 8 ingredients in large bowl until fluffy. Mix in reserved 2 tablespoons minced orange peel. Add eggs 1 at a time, beating well after each addition. Sift flour, baking soda and baking powder into medium bowl. Mix half and half and lemon juice in small bowl. Beat dry ingredients alternately with half and half mixture into butter mixture, beginning and ending with dry ingredients. Mix in currants. Pour batter into prepared pan. Bake until toothpick inserted into center comes out clean, about 50 minutes. (Cake will not rise to top of pan.) Cool cake 20 minutes. Run small sharp knife around pan sides to loosen. Turn cake out onto rack; cool. Peel off paper. (*Can be prepared up to 1 day ahead. Cover syrup and cake separately and let stand at room temperature.*)

For frosting: Melt chocolate in top of double boiler over simmering water, stirring occasionally until smooth. Cool to barely lukewarm. Using electric mixer, beat butter and cream cheese until light. Add chocolate and ¼ cup honey syrup and beat until smooth and light. Chill until thick enough to spread, stirring occasionally, about 20 minutes.

Cut cake horizontally in half. Place bottom layer cut side up on platter. Brush with ¼ cup honey syrup. Spread 1¼ cups frosting over. Brush remaining ¼ cup syrup over cut side of top cake layer. Place cake cut side down atop filled layer. Set aside ⅔ cup frosting for garnish. Spread remaining frosting over top and sides of cake. Press almonds around sides. Spoon remaining ⅔ cup frosting into pastry bag fitted with small star tip. Pipe frosting decoratively around top edge of cake. Chill cake until frosting sets, about 1 hour. Garnish with orange slices. (*Can be prepared 1 day ahead. Cover and refrigerate. Let cake stand 2 hours at room temperature before serving.*)

Raspberry and Coffee Tiramisù

An unexpected combination of ingredients updates the classic Italian dessert. It is presented in individual servings here, but the lady-fingers, espresso and filling can be layered in a large dish and offered with the sauce on the side.

6 servings

Ladyfinger Rounds
½ cup all purpose flour
½ teaspoon finely ground coffee (preferably espresso)
3 extra-large eggs, separated, room temperature
5 tablespoons sugar
½ teaspoon vanilla extract

Powdered sugar

Filling
3 tablespoons framboise eau-de-vie (clear raspberry brandy)
1 tablespoon instant espresso powder or instant coffee granules

2 8-ounce packages cream cheese (preferably old-fashioned, low-salt cream cheese), room temperature
⅔ cup powdered sugar
1 6-ounce basket raspberries or 1½ cups frozen unsweetened, thawed, drained

¾ cup freshly brewed strong coffee (preferably espresso), room temperature
3 tablespoons sugar
Additional powdered sugar
Raspberry-Brandy Sauce (see recipe)
Fresh mint

For ladyfinger rounds: Preheat oven to 350°F. Line 2 cookie sheets with parchment. Mix flour and ground coffee in small bowl. Using electric mixer, beat egg yolks and 4 tablespoons sugar in medium bowl until thick and slowly dissolving ribbon forms when beaters are lifted, about 4 minutes. Beat in vanilla. Mix in dry ingredients (batter will be thick). Using electric mixer fitted with clean dry beaters, beat egg whites until thick and foamy. Add remaining 1 tablespoon sugar and beat until whites are stiff but not dry. Fold beaten egg whites into yolk mixture in 2 additions.

Drop batter by rounded tablespoons (8 per sheet) onto prepared cookie sheets, spacing evenly. Sift powdered sugar thickly over rounds. Bake until rounds are golden brown on edges, about 16 minutes. Cool in pan on rack. Remove ladyfinger rounds from parchment. (*Can be prepared 1 day ahead. Store in single layer in airtight container.*)

For filling: Combine framboise and espresso powder in small bowl. Stir until espresso dissolves. Using electric mixer, beat cream cheese and ⅔ cup powdered sugar until light and fluffy. Beat in coffee mixture. Fold in 1 cup raspberries. Let filling stand at room temperature.

Combine coffee and 3 tablespoons sugar. Stir until sugar dissolves. Spoon 1 scant tablespoon coffee mixture over flat side of 1 ladyfinger round. Place coffee side up on plate. Spread ⅓ cup filling atop round. Spoon 1 scant tablespoon coffee mixture over flat side of second ladyfinger round. Place flat side down atop filling. Sprinkle with powdered sugar. Repeat with remaining ladyfinger rounds, coffee, filling and powdered sugar. Spoon raspberry sauce around desserts. Garnish with remaining raspberries and fresh mint and serve.

Raspberry-Brandy Sauce

Makes about 1¼ cups

1 10-ounce package frozen raspberries in syrup, thawed

2 tablespoons framboise eau-de-vie (clear raspberry brandy)

Puree raspberries and syrup in processor. Strain into small bowl in remove seeds. Stir in eau-de-vie. (*Can be prepared 2 days ahead. Cover and refrigerate.*)

Lemon-Lattice White Chocolate Cake

The contrast of the subtle white chocolate cake and frosting with a tart-sweet lemon curd filling is superb.

12 servings

Lemon Curd
¾ cup fresh lemon juice
2 tablespoons cornstarch
1 cup plus 2 tablespoons sugar
3 large eggs
6 large egg yolks
½ cup plus 1 tablespoon unsalted butter, cut into small pieces
2 tablespoons grated lemon peel

Frosting
2¼ cups whipping cream
4½ ounces imported white chocolate (such as Lindt), chopped
¾ teaspoon vanilla extract

Cake
2¾ cups sifted all purpose flour
1 teaspoon baking powder
¾ teaspoon salt

4 ounces imported white chocolate (such as Lindt), chopped
1 cup whipping cream
½ cup plus 2 tablespoons milk
1 teaspoon vanilla extract

½ cup (1 stick) unsalted butter, room temperature
2 cups sugar
4 large eggs, separated

For lemon curd: Combine lemon juice and cornstarch in heavy medium saucepan, stirring until cornstarch dissolves. Whisk in remaining ingredients. Cook over medium heat until mixture is thick and smooth and just begins to boil, stirring constantly, about 7 minutes. Transfer to medium bowl. Place plastic wrap directly on surface of curd to prevent skin from forming. Refrigerate until chilled, about 6 hours. (*Can be prepared 2 days ahead.*)

For frosting: Combine ½ cup cream and chocolate in heavy small saucepan. Stir over low heat until chocolate melts and mixture is smooth. Transfer to large bowl. Whisk in remaining 1¾ cups cream and vanilla. Refrigerate until well chilled, about 6 hours. (*Can be prepared up to 1 day ahead.*)

For cake: Position rack in center of oven and preheat to 350°F. Butter three 9-inch-diameter cake pans with 1½-inch-high sides. Line bottoms with waxed paper. Butter paper. Dust pans with flour; tap out excess. Sift flour, baking powder and salt together into medium bowl. Repeat sifting.

Stir chocolate and ½ cup cream in heavy medium saucepan over low heat until chocolate melts and mixture is smooth. Mix in remaining ½ cup whipping cream, milk and vanilla extract.

Using electric mixer, beat butter and 1 cup sugar in large bowl until fluffy. Beat in yolks. Stir dry ingredients into butter mixture alternately with white chocolate mixture, beginning and ending with dry ingredients. Using electric mixer fitted with clean dry beaters, beat egg whites in medium bowl to soft peaks. Gradually beat in remaining 1 cup sugar. Continue beating until stiff but not dry. Fold whites into cake batter in 2 additions. Divide batter among prepared cake pans. Bake until tester inserted in center comes out clean and cakes are beginning to pull away from sides of pans, about 24 minutes. Cool cakes in pans on racks 10 minutes. Turn cakes out onto racks, peel off waxed paper and cool. (*Can be prepared 4 hours ahead. Cover; let stand at room temperature.*)

Using electric mixer, beat frosting in another large bowl until stiff peaks form. Place 1 cake layer on platter. Spread ⅔ cup lemon curd evenly atop cake layer. Spread ¾ cup frosting atop curd. Top with second cake layer. Spread cake with ⅔ cup curd, then with ¾ cup frosting. Top with third cake layer. Frost top and sides of entire cake evenly with 3 cups frosting.

Place remaining lemon curd in pastry bag fitted with no. 2 star tip. Pipe circle of curd around top of cake, ½ inch from edge. Pipe evenly spaced diagonal lines inside circle, creating lattice pattern. (Reserve remaining curd for another use.) Spoon remaining frosting into clean pastry bag fitted with no. 2 star tip. Pipe ruffled border around top and bottom edges of cake. (*Can be prepared 6 hours ahead. Chill.*) Let stand at room temperature 30 minutes before serving.

Spiced Prune-Almond "Coffee" Cake

Terrific when served with vanilla or coffee ice cream, and a very appealing breakfast or snack cake on its own.

10 servings

Cake
- ¾ cup whole unblanched almonds, toasted, finely chopped
- 1 cup buttermilk
- 2½ tablespoons instant coffee granules
- 1 teaspoon vanilla extract
- ¼ teaspoon almond extract
- 2½ cups unbleached all purpose flour
- 2 teaspoons baking powder
- 1 teaspoon baking soda
- 1 teaspoon ground cinnamon
- 1 teaspoon salt
- ¼ teaspoon ground cloves

- 1 cup (2 sticks) unsalted butter, room temperature
- 1 cup sugar
- 3 extra-large eggs, room temperature
- 1 cup (about 6 ounces) pitted prunes, coarsely chopped
- 1 tablespoon grated orange peel

Glaze
- ½ cup firmly packed dark brown sugar
- ¼ cup (½ stick) unsalted butter
- ¼ cup whipping cream
- 1 teaspoon instant coffee granules

Orange slices (optional)
Cinnamon stick (optional)

For cake: Position rack in center of oven and preheat to 350°F. Generously butter 10-inch (12-cup) tube pan. Sprinkle half of almonds into pan. Tilt to coat bottom and halfway up sides with nuts (do not tap out excess). Combine buttermilk, coffee granules, vanilla and almond extracts in small bowl. Stir until coffee dissolves. Sift flour, baking powder, baking soda, ground cinnamon, salt and ground cloves into medium bowl.

Using electric mixer, cream butter and sugar in large bowl until light and fluffy. Add eggs 1 at a time, beating well after each addition. Slowly mix in dry ingredients alternately with buttermilk mixture, beginning and ending with dry ingredients. Mix in prunes and orange peel. Pour batter into prepared pan. Sprinkle with remaining almonds. Bake until tester inserted into center of cake comes out clean, about 50 minutes. Cool 30 minutes in pan on rack. Turn cake out onto rack. Quickly turn upright onto platter and cool until just warm.

For glaze: Combine brown sugar, butter and cream in heavy small saucepan. Stir over medium-high heat until butter melts. Boil 2 minutes. Mix in instant coffee granules. Cool slightly. Drizzle glaze over cake.

Garnish cake with orange slices and cinnamon stick if desired and serve warm or at room temperature.

Chocolate Cheesecake

12 servings

Filling
- 2½ pounds cream cheese, room temperature (very soft)
- 1¾ cups sugar
- 1 cup unsweetened cocoa powder, sifted
- 3 large eggs, room temperature
- ½ cup whipping cream
- 2 tablespoons coffee liqueur
- 1½ tablespoons Frangelico (hazelnut liqueur)
- 1 teaspoon vanilla extract

Chocolate Glaze
- ¼ cup coffee liqueur
- ¼ cup Frangelico (hazelnut liqueur)
- 2 tablespoons dark rum
- 12 ounces bittersweet (not unsweetened) or semisweet chocolate, chopped
- ¼ cup whipping cream
- ¼ cup (½ stick) unsalted butter

For filling: Position rack in center of oven and preheat to 300°F. Line bottom of 9-inch-diameter springform pan with 2¾-inch-high sides with waxed paper. Spray paper with nonstick vegetable oil spray. Using electric mixer, beat cream cheese and sugar in large bowl on low speed until smooth. Gradually mix in cocoa. Beat in eggs 1 at a time. Gradually add cream, coffee liqueur, Frangelico and vanilla and beat until mixture is smooth.

Transfer filling to prepared pan. Bake until outer 3 inches of cake puff and center is gently set but moist looking, about 1 hour 30 minutes. Cool on rack. Cover and refrigerate until cake is well chilled, at least 6 hours. (*Cheesecake can be prepared up to 1 day ahead.*)

For glaze: Boil coffee liqueur, Frangelico and rum in heavy medium saucepan until reduced to ¼ cup, about 3 minutes. Reduce heat to low and add chocolate, cream and butter. Stir until mixture is smooth. Cool until mixture is thick but still pourable, stirring occasionally, about 45 minutes.

Using small sharp knife, cut around pan sides to loosen cake. Release and remove pan sides. Pour chocolate glaze over cake. Spread smoothly over top and sides, covering completely. Chill until chocolate is firm, at least 2 hours.

Invert cake onto serving platter. Peel off paper. Smooth top. Using warm knife, cut into wedges and serve.

Chocolate Pecan Torte

10 servings

Cake
- 6 ounces bittersweet (not unsweetened) or semisweet chocolate, chopped
- ¾ cup (1½ sticks) unsalted butter, room temperature
- ¾ cup sugar
- 1½ teaspoons vanilla extract
- ½ teaspoon salt
- 6 large eggs, separated
- 1½ cups chopped toasted pecans
- ¼ cup all purpose flour

Icing
- ½ cup whipping cream
- 1 teaspoon instant coffee powder
- 4 ounces bittersweet (not unsweetened) or semisweet chocolate, chopped
- ½ cup apricot jam

For cake: Preheat oven to 350°F. Butter 9-inch-diameter springform pan with 2¾-inch-high sides. Line bottom with foil. Butter foil. Dust pan with flour; tap out excess. Melt chocolate in top of double boiler over barely simmering water, stirring until smooth. Cool. Using electric mixer, cream butter, sugar, vanilla and salt in large bowl until light. Add yolks 1 at a time, beating well after each addition. Mix in chocolate. Toss pecans with flour and mix into batter. Using electric mixer fitted with clean dry beaters, beat whites in another large bowl to soft peaks. Fold whites into batter in 2 additions.

Pour batter into prepared pan. Bake until tester inserted in center of cake comes out clean, about 45 minutes. Cool cake 20 minutes in pan on rack. Release pan sides. Turn cake out onto rack and cool completely. Remove foil.

For icing: Bring cream to simmer in heavy medium saucepan over medium heat. Reduce heat to low. Add coffee powder, then chocolate and stir until smooth. Cool to room temperature, 30 minutes.

Meanwhile, melt jam in heavy small saucepan over medium heat, stirring frequently. Strain jam. Brush over top and sides of cake. Let stand 30 minutes.

Pour icing over cake. Smooth over top and sides of cake using icing spatula. Refrigerate until icing sets, about 15 minutes. (*Can be prepared 1 day ahead. Cover and refrigerate. Let stand 2 hours at room temperature before serving.*)

Devil's Food Cake

Grated raw beet is the surprise ingredient that makes this luscious cake especially dense and moist.

8 servings

Cake

2 cups all purpose flour
1¾ cups sugar
¾ cup unsweetened cocoa powder
1½ teaspoons baking powder
1 teaspoon salt
½ teaspoon baking soda
1½ cups buttermilk
3 large eggs
1 teaspoon vanilla extract

¾ cup (1½ sticks) unsalted butter, melted, cooled
½ cup sour cream
½ cup grated raw beets

Frosting

1 cup whipping cream
14 ounces bittersweet (not unsweetened) or semisweet chocolate, chopped
2 tablespoons light corn syrup

For cake: Preheat oven to 350°F. Butter 10-inch-diameter cake pan with 2-inch-high sides. Line bottom with parchment; butter parchment. Sift flour, sugar, unsweetened cocoa powder, baking powder, salt and baking soda into large bowl of electric mixer. Add buttermilk, eggs and vanilla extract and beat until blended. Mix in ¾ cup melted butter and sour cream. Stir in grated beets. Pour batter into prepared pan. Bake until toothpick inserted into center of cake comes out clean, about 65 minutes. Transfer to rack and cool 10 minutes. Turn cake out onto rack and cool completely.

For frosting: Scald whipping cream in heavy medium saucepan over medium heat. Remove from heat. Add chopped chocolate and stir until melted and smooth. Mix in light corn syrup. Transfer to medium bowl. Refrigerate frosting until just spreadable, about 15 minutes.

Cut cooled cake into 2 even layers. Spread top of 1 cake layer with ½ cup frosting. Top with second cake layer. Spread top and sides with remaining frosting. (*Can be prepared 1 day ahead. Cover with cake dome and store at room temperature.*) Cut into wedges and serve.

Miniature Chocolate Cakes with Chocolate Sauce and Port Sabayon

8 servings

Cakes

3 ounces unsweetened chocolate, chopped
3 ounces bittersweet (not unsweetened) or semisweet chocolate, chopped

½ cup (1 stick) unsalted butter, room temperature
¾ cup plus 2 tablespoons sugar
4 extra-large eggs, separated
6 tablespoons apricot jam
3 tablespoons Port wine
½ cup coarsely ground pine nuts
6 tablespoons all purpose flour
¼ cup cake flour

Chocolate Sauce

6 tablespoons whipping cream
6 ounces bittersweet (not unsweetened) or semisweet chocolate, chopped

Port Sabayon

6 egg yolks
½ cup Port wine
⅓ cup sugar
½ cup whipping cream

2 tablespoons toasted pine nuts

For cakes: Preheat oven to 325°F. Butter eight ¾-cup custard cups. Melt both chocolates in top of double boiler over simmering water, stirring until smooth. Cool melted chocolates slightly.

Using electric mixer, cream butter and sugar in large bowl until light. Blend in yolks, jam and Port. Stir in melted chocolates. Mix in pine nuts and both flours. Using electric mixer fitted with clean dry beaters, beat whites in medium bowl until stiff but not dry. Fold half of whites into chocolate mixture. Fold in remaining beaten egg whites.

Place prepared custard cups on heavy large cookie sheet. Divide batter among cups. Bake until cakes puff and toothpick inserted in centers comes out with moist crumbs still attached, about 25 minutes. Transfer to rack and cool (cakes will fall in center). Run small sharp knife around sides of cups to loosen cakes. Turn out onto platter. (*Can be prepared up to 1 day ahead. Cover cakes and let stand at room temperature.*)

For chocolate sauce: Bring cream to simmer in heavy small saucepan over medium-low heat. Add chocolate and stir until melted. Set aside.

For Port sabayon: Whisk yolks with Port and sugar in medium metal bowl to blend. Set bowl over saucepan of simmering water and whisk Port mixture until candy thermometer registers 140°F. Continue cooking 3 minutes, whisking constantly. Add whipping cream and whisk until mixture is heated through. Remove bowl from over water.

Transfer 1 cake to each of 8 plates. Spoon sabayon around each cake. Pour chocolate sauce over cakes. Sprinkle with pine nuts and serve.

 Cookies

Pine Nut-Almond Macaroons

Chewy cookies that are great with ice cream, espresso or a glass of Marsala.

Makes about 22

¼ cup Marsala
3 tablespoons dried currants

¾ cup toasted slivered almonds
½ cup toasted pine nuts
⅔ cup sugar

1 tablespoon all purpose flour
1 large egg white
⅛ teaspoon (generous) almond extract
1 cup (about) pine nuts (4½ ounces)

Preheat oven to 350°F. Line large cookie sheet with foil. Combine Marsala and currants in heavy small saucepan. Cook over medium heat until liquid evaporates, about 5 minutes. Cool completely.

Finely grind almonds and ½ cup toasted pine nuts with sugar and flour in processor. Mix egg white with extract in medium bowl. Add to processor and blend until dough forms ball. Return dough to bowl. Mix in currants. Shape dough between palms into ¾-inch-diameter balls. Roll in 1 cup pine nuts to cover, pressing to adhere. Flatten each to 1½-inch round. Space evenly on cookie sheet. Bake until golden brown, about 15 minutes. Cool slightly. Remove cookies from foil using metal spatula and cool on rack. (*Can be prepared 4 days ahead. Store in airtight container at room temperature.*)

Fudgy Brownies

Makes 12

Brownies
1½ cups all purpose flour
2 teaspoons baking powder
1 teaspoon salt
1 cup (2 sticks) unsalted butter
6 ounces unsweetened chocolate, chopped
5 large eggs
2¼ cups sugar
2 teaspoons vanilla

1 cup chopped walnuts

Frosting
½ cup (1 stick) unsalted butter
2 ounces unsweetened chocolate, chopped
¼ cup unsweetened cocoa powder
4 tablespoons milk
1 teaspoon vanilla
2 cups powdered sugar

For brownies: Preheat oven to 350°F. Butter 9 × 13-inch baking pan with 2-inch-high sides. Combine first 3 ingredients in small bowl. Stir butter and chocolate in heavy small saucepan over low heat until melted and smooth. Beat eggs, sugar and vanilla in large bowl to blend. Stir in warm chocolate mixture, then dry ingredients. Mix in nuts. Pour batter into prepared pan. Bake until toothpick inserted into center comes out with moist crumbs attached, about 30 minutes. Cool completely.

For frosting: Stir butter and chocolate in small saucepan over low heat until melted. Stir in cocoa powder, 2 tablespoons milk and vanilla. Whisk in powdered sugar. Mix in enough remaining milk to form smooth frosting.

Frost brownies. Cut into 12 pieces. (*Can be prepared 1 day ahead. Store in airtight container at room temperature.*)

Old-fashioned Sugar Cookies

Makes about 2 dozen

2 cups all purpose flour
½ teaspoon baking powder
½ teaspoon baking soda
¼ teaspoon salt
½ cup solid vegetable shortening
¾ cup sugar

1 egg
1 teaspoon vanilla
1 teaspoon grated orange peel
3 tablespoons milk

Additional sugar

Preheat oven to 375°F. Sift 2 cups flour, ½ teaspoon baking powder, ½ teaspoon baking soda and ¼ teaspoon salt into medium bowl. Using electric mixer, cream ½ cup shortening and ¾ cup sugar in large bowl. Beat in 1 egg, 1 teaspoon vanilla and 1 teaspoon orange peel. Mix in dry ingredients alternately with milk, beginning and ending with dry ingredients.

Lightly grease 2 large cookie sheets. Roll dough out on lightly floured surface to ⅛-inch thickness. Cut 3-inch-diameter rounds using cookie or biscuit cutter. Transfer dough rounds to prepared cookie sheets. Gather and reroll scraps. Cut additional cookies. Sprinkle cookies with sugar. Bake cookies until golden brown on edges, about 14 minutes. Transfer to rack and cool completely. (*Can be prepared 1 week ahead. Store in airtight container.*)

Date Crumb Bars

Makes 24

Filling
1 pound pitted dates
1 cup firmly packed brown sugar
²/₃ cup water
1 teaspoon vanilla extract

Crust
1½ cups old-fashioned oats

1½ cups all purpose flour
1 cup firmly packed brown sugar
½ teaspoon baking soda
1 cup (2 sticks) chilled unsalted butter, cut into small pieces

For filling: Combine all ingredients in medium saucepan. Bring to simmer, stirring to dissolve sugar. Simmer 1 minute. Puree mixture in processor. Cool.

For crust: Preheat oven to 350°F. Butter 9 × 13-inch baking pan. Mix oats, flour, sugar and soda in medium bowl. Add butter and rub with fingertips until mixture resembles coarse crumbs. Firmly press half of crumb mixture into bottom of prepared baking pan.

Spread filling over crust. Sprinkle remaining crumb mixture over filling. Bake until topping is golden brown, about 38 minutes. Cool in pan. (*Can be prepared 1 day ahead. Cover and let stand at room temperature.*) Cut into squares.

Island Macaroons

These cookies have a wonderful texture: chewy yet crunchy—just like a candy bar.

Makes about 24

3 cups sweetened flaked coconut
1 cup unsalted macadamia nuts, chopped

²/₃ cup sweetened condensed milk
1 teaspoon vanilla extract

2 egg whites
Pinch of salt

6 ounces bittersweet (not unsweetened) or semisweet chocolate, chopped, melted

Preheat oven to 350°F. Place coconut and macadamia nuts on large cookie sheet. Bake until lightly toasted, stirring frequently, about 12 minutes. Cool coconut and nuts completely. Maintain oven temperature.

Line 2 large cookie sheets with parchment paper. Grease parchment. Combine condensed milk and vanilla in large bowl. Mix in coconut and macadamia nuts thoroughly. Using electric mixer, beat egg whites and salt until stiff but not dry. Fold whites into coconut mixture. Drop batter by rounded tablespoons onto prepared cookie sheets. Bake until macaroons just turn golden brown around edges, about 14 minutes. Cool completely on cookie sheets.

Line another cookie sheet with waxed paper. Dip cookie bottoms into melted chocolate. Place cookies, chocolate side down, on prepared cookie sheet. Refrigerate until chocolate is set, about 15 minutes. (*Can be prepared 4 days ahead. Store cookies in airtight container in refrigerator.*)

Double Chocolate Brownies

Makes 16

Filling
- ¼ cup purchased chocolate syrup
- 2 ounces semisweet chocolate, chopped, or chocolate chips
- 1 8-ounce package cream cheese, room temperature
- 1 large egg
- ¼ cup semisweet chocolate chips
- 1 tablespoon all purpose flour

Chocolate Batter
- 1 cup (2 sticks) unsalted butter, room temperature
- 1¼ cups sugar
- 4 large eggs
- 1 teaspoon vanilla extract
- 1⅓ cups all purpose flour
- ¾ cup unsweetened cocoa powder
- ¼ teaspoon baking powder

Glaze
- 6 ounces semisweet chocolate, chopped, or chocolate chips
- 1 tablespoon vegetable oil

For filling: Combine syrup and 2 ounces chopped chocolate in heavy small saucepan. Stir over low heat until chocolate melts; cool. Beat cream cheese and egg in medium bowl. Stir in chocolate mixture. Blend in ¼ cup chocolate chips and flour. Set filling aside.

For batter: Preheat oven to 350°F. Grease 9-inch square baking pan with 2-inch-high sides. Line bottom with waxed paper. Butter waxed paper. Using electric mixer, beat butter and sugar in large bowl until fluffy. Add eggs 1 at a time, beating well after each addition. Beat in vanilla. Sift flour, cocoa and baking powder into medium bowl. Stir dry ingredients into butter mixture.

Spoon half of chocolate batter into prepared pan. Top with filling. Spread remaining batter over. Bake brownies until toothpick inserted in center comes out clean, about 40 minutes. Transfer to rack. Cool 5 minutes. Run small sharp knife around edges of pan to loosen. Cool completely in pan.

For glaze: Melt 6 ounces chocolate with vegetable oil in heavy small saucepan over low heat, stirring constantly.

Cut cooled brownies into sixteen 2-inch squares. Transfer to rack. Spoon warm glaze over brownies. Let stand until glaze sets. Arrange on platter.

Lemon and Anise Sugar Twists

These easy-to-make treats are delicious on their own or with fresh fruit. Keep them in mind for a hostess gift.

Makes 12

Sugar
- 1 sheet frozen puff pastry (half of 17½-ounce package), thawed
- 1 egg beaten with 1 teaspoon milk (glaze)
- 3 tablespoons sugar
- 1 teaspoon grated lemon peel
- 2 teaspoons aniseed

Preheat oven to 350°F. Sprinkle work surface with sugar. Set pastry atop sugar and roll out to thickness of ⅛ inch. Brush with egg glaze. Combine 3 tablespoons sugar and lemon peel in small bowl. Sprinkle over pastry. Sprinkle with aniseed. Cut pastry crosswise into 1-inch-wide strips. Pick up each pastry strip, twist several times and place on ungreased cookie sheet, pressing ends onto sheet. Bake until golden brown and crisp, about 20 minutes. Cool on rack.

Chunky Nutty Brownies

Makes about 16

½ cup (1 stick) unsalted butter
3 ounces unsweetened chocolate (such as Baker's), chopped
1¼ cups sugar
2 eggs
½ cup all purpose flour

⅔ cup coarsely chopped toasted pecans (about 3 ounces)
2 ounces imported bittersweet (not unsweetened) or semisweet chocolate, cut into chunks
2 ounces imported milk chocolate, cut into chunks

Preheat oven to 350°F. Butter and flour 9 × 9-inch baking pan with 2-inch-high sides. Melt butter and unsweetened chocolate in heavy small saucepan over low heat, stirring constantly. Pour chocolate mixture into large bowl. Whisk in sugar and eggs. Mix in flour, then nuts and chocolate chunks. Pour batter into prepared pan. Bake until tester inserted into center comes out with moist crumbs attached, about 30 minutes. Cool brownies in pan on rack. (*Can be prepared 2 days ahead. Cover and chill. Bring to room temperature.*) Cut into squares.

Double Lemon Bars

Makes 24

1½ cups all purpose flour
½ cup powdered sugar
¾ cup (1½ sticks) butter, cut into pieces, room temperature

4 eggs
1½ cups sugar

½ cup fresh lemon juice
1 tablespoon plus 1 teaspoon all purpose flour
1 tablespoon grated lemon peel

Powdered sugar

Preheat oven to 350°F. Combine 1½ cups flour and ½ cup powdered sugar in large bowl. Add butter and cut in until mixture resembles coarse meal. Press mixture into bottom of 9 × 13 × 2-inch baking dish. Bake until golden brown, about 20 minutes. Remove from oven. Maintain oven temperature.

Beat eggs, 1½ cups sugar, lemon juice, 1 tablespoon plus 1 teaspoon flour and lemon peel in medium bowl to blend. Pour into crust. Bake until mixture is set, about 20 minutes. Cool completely.

Cut into 24 bars. Sift powdered sugar over top before serving.

Index

News '91

The Year of Food and Entertaining in Review

Trends & New Products

Foods & Info by Mail

Books

Restaurants & People

Getaways

For the Kitchen & Table

Diet News

🍎 *Trends & New Products*

EARTH SAVER

A round of applause goes to the Hard Rock Cafe in Las Vegas. It's the latest member of the worldwide chain's Save the Planet program in which all glass, cardboard and plastics are recycled, Styrofoam is forbidden and no food preservatives are used. (Hard Rock Cafe, 4475 Paradise Road, Las Vegas, NV 89109; telephone 702-733-8400.)

BURPEE GOES HIGH FASHION

There's a silk crepe de chine scarf from the Echo Design Group that makes a charming gift for gardeners and food lovers alike. Printed with images of antique seed packets from Burpee, it's a nifty accessory indeed. The scarf is found at department stores, such as Saks Fifth Avenue, and specialty shops for about $110.

T TIME

At your child's next birthday bash, instead of handing out the usual grab bag of party favors, why not give the kiddies "cake" T-shirts? The heavy-weight cotton tops are available in children's sizes XS (2 to 4), S (6 to 8), M (10 to 12) and L (14 to 16). Send a check or money order for $16 per shirt to Janet Dennis, 52 High Street, Charlestown, MA 02129; 617-241-7334.

FAUX FOOD

Fruits and vegetables have been an inspiration for still-life artists from time immemorial. They are also the preferred subject matter for American sculptor Franklin Gilliam. His trompe l'oeil masterpieces are carved from stone or cast in bronze. They're available through the Carolyn Hill Gallery, 109 Spring Street, New York, NY 10012. Call 212-226-4611 for more information about selection and prices.

GOING GREEN

We're big fans of the Seventh Generation catalog. It lists over 300 environmentally friendly products. Try the heavy-duty 100 percent biodegradable paper garbage bags, organic coffee, cellulose bags, vegetable-based dishwashing liquid and more. For a catalog, call them at 800-456-1177.

MARSALA FOR SIPPING

This popular Italian wine is for more than making sauces—it's a terrific post-prandial drink. Marsala Superiore from De Bartoli is one of the best. Wood-aged for 20 years, it's rich, mildly sweet and has complex nutty flavors. Serve with a fancy dessert or simply accompanied by cheese, fruit and walnuts. Find it for about $33 per 750-ml bottle at better wine stores.

WEARABLE FOOD

Catfish earrings. Table-setting cuff links. A carrot pin. These and other gastronomic jewelry selections will satisfy food cravings at no calorie cost. The sales benefit The James Beard Foundation, a nonprofit organization that supports the growth of American food and wine education. For a "menu" of jewelry styles, contact The James Beard Collection, 14509 Falling Leaf Court, Darnestown, MD 20878.

AT YOUR SERVICE

Like the traditional American country furniture it's patterned after, the "Madeline Buffet" is sure to stand the test of time: The piece is handcrafted, right down to the joints secured with wooden pegs. It's part of a new line of furniture from The Farm House Collection. For additional information, call 208-788-3187.

NEAT SEAT

Can a dining chair be both comfortable and good-looking? The people at Angelo Donghia Furniture/Textiles have the answer. Called Studio X, the stylish seat is covered in cotton pebble cloth by Richard Giglio; color patterns range from black and ecru to ecru combined with gold, indigo, khaki or chalk. Available to the trade. For more information, call 800-DONGHIA.

PRIZE CATCH

A couple of years ago we were dazzled by Inner Beauty's Real Hot Sauce (made with scorching Scotch Bonnet peppers). Now this saucy company from Cambridge, Massachusetts, has come up with another winner. Blue Marlin Fish & Meat Sauce is a savory, tropical-style concoction of tamarind and bananas that's perfect for marinades and dipping. The price in specialty stores around the country is about $5.99 for a 6.8-ounce bottle.

TRUE BREW

Ginger lovers will flip for a zingy new drink called Reed's Original Ginger Brew. Its assertive bite makes most other ginger ales taste watered down. This nonalcoholic beverage has no sugar (it's sweetened with honey and fruit juices), no preservatives and no artificial flavorings. The 12-ounce bottles cost about ninety-five cents each and can be found at specialty foods stores nationwide. Call 213-281-4723 for a location near you.

RED ROVER

Hikers and bikers will appreciate the bright red, lightweight, durable aluminum flasks from The Civilized Traveller. A protective internal finish keeps refreshments safe, while a carabiner hook makes sure the canteen stays put. There are two sizes: 1 liter and .75 liter. They are $21 and $20 respectively (plus shipping) from The Civilized Traveller, 1072 Third Avenue, New York, NY 10021; 212-758-8305.

WATER BREAK

Clearly Canadian, a new sparkling mineral water in delectable flavors (like Western Loganberry, Orchard Peach, Mountain Blackberry and Wild Cherry), is a refreshing change of pace from the usual soft drinks. An 11-ounce bottle sells for about $1.25; a 23-ounce bottle is about $1.75. Available at specialty foods stores and selected supermarkets nationwide.

GRATE IDEA

Keep delicate foods like fish fillets and vegetables out of the fire with Griffo's Mark IV grill. With closely arranged holes, wide handles and an easy-to-clean porcelain finish, it works great atop your trusty barbecue (rectangular and half-circle models are available). Buy one for about $30 at Crate & Barrel stores or through *The Chef's Catalog* at 800-338-3232.

❦ Foods & Info by Mail

OATS AND MORE

Cafe Fanny granola—made under the watchful eye of renowned chef Alice Waters—is a terrific, not-too-sweet blend of oats, honey, almonds, raisins, and sunflower and sesame seeds. It's a bargain at $3.75 per pound; there's a five-pound minimum for mail orders, but the mixture freezes beautifully. (Cafe Fanny, 1619 Fifth Street, Berkeley, CA 94710; call 800-441-5413.)

SAY CHEESECAKE

People who like their cheesecake with a little something special will love the Marionberry version made by It's From Oregon. Considered the "Cadillac of blackberries," this rare berry adds just the right touch of sweetness and color. A 2-pound cake costs $19 and can be ordered by calling 800-247-0727. The best cheesecake for purists? A favorite is the creamy, dreamy one from Eli's Chicago's Finest. Pre-sliced for easy entertaining, the 3½-pound cake is $27; call 800-999-8300 to order one by mail.

FABULOUS FROMAGE

In France, the Androuë family is famous for their hand-selected farmhouse cheeses. That fame is sure to spread, because now the Androuës are exporting to the United States. Try a creamy Livarot or an assertive Bleu de Laqueille. Livarot is $8.75 for about ⅔ pound; and a 1-pound wheel of Bleu de Laqueille costs $15.99, plus shipping. To order these cheeses, call Balducci's at 212-673-2600.

TROPICAL TREATS

The Exotic Fruit Basket from Frieda's, Inc., makes a great gift for almost anyone—from the discriminating gourmand to your favorite health-and-fitness fan. The eight- and five-pound baskets feature such uncommon delights as cherimoyas, passion fruit, Asian pears and horned melons. Plus,

they're packed so the fruit arrives in just-picked condition. The larger basket is $76, the smaller $59, and price includes second-day delivery service. To order, telephone 800-241-1771 (in California, 213-627-2981).

GAME TIME

Planning a dinner party but had it with chicken and chops? Bored with beef? Try the naturally raised quail, pheasant and chukar partridge from Wylie Hill Farm for a change—they're terrific for an elegant menu. The smoked pheasant are $20 each; fresh pheasant, $16 each; fresh quail, eight for $28; fresh partridge, two for $18. Prices include postage but not handling. (Wylie Hill Farm, P.O. Box 35, Craftsbury Common, VT 05827-35BA 802-586-2887.)

EGGS-CITING!

There is a semisweet chocolate dinosaur egg from Cocolat that will delight chocolate lovers of all ages. Milk chocolate and bittersweet baby dinos (ten in all) nest inside a large milk chocolate egg wrapped in gold foil. The set is $19.95 from Cocolat, 1787 Sabre Street, Hayward, CA 94545; 800-COCOLAT.

TIPPING KNOW-HOW

Tips on Tipping, a plastic, credit-card-size guide, shows you whom to tip and how much. It's invaluable if you travel or dine out frequently. Three cards cost $2.50. To order, send a check payable to Abelexpress, 240-V East Main Street, Carnegie, PA 15106.

HAZELNUT HEAVEN

If toffee is a favorite around your house, then you'll want to try this delicious version from Pacific Hazelnut Farms in Oregon. Flavored with ground hazelnuts, the buttery rich toffee is dipped in milk chocolate and

then coated with more hazelnuts. A four-ounce bag is $2.65, plus shipping; a six-ounce gift box is $4.50. To order, call 800-634-7344.

BOTTOMS UP

The name says it all: The Chocolate Bottom Brandied Pecan Tart is one decadent dessert. The seven-inch tart costs $19.95 and serves 6 to 8; the nine-inch version is $24.95 and serves from 8 to 12. To order either, telephone Epicurean Fantasys toll free at 800-688-7400.

JUST DUCKY

Magret—a choice cut of duck breast—makes a refined repast, indeed. Whether roasted, grilled or sautéed, it's moist and succulent—never dry. A two-pound package of fresh magret is $24, plus shipping costs, from D'Artagnan. To order, telephone toll free 800-DARTAGN.

HONEY OF A MUSTARD

After 139 years in the business, Honey Acres has learned a thing or two about honey. They're also pretty quick studies when it comes to mustard. Now they've paired the two to create a line of excellent honey-mustard blends: tangy-sweet Honeydill; zesty Honey-hot and robust Honeygrain. A 6.5-ounce jar is about $2.39, plus shipping; phone 800-558-7745 to order.

FRESH FROM THE OVEN

In Sicily, *scalette* means "little step ladder" and is the name for a traditional bread that's shaped by hand and baked in a brick hearth. Alesci's scalette bread is still handmade, but now all you do is put the loaf into the oven for 15 minutes and you'll have fresh-baked bread that no one can refuse. A sampler of two 1-pound loaves and two half-pound loaves costs $12.50, including second-day air delivery. Call 800-88-DOUGH or, in Ohio, 216-663-1860.

LIGHT LINKS

Sausages made from poultry and game are a delightful change of pace from their heartier cousins of pork or beef. We like the fresh smoked chicken and apple links made by Bruce Aidells, plus the chicken and turkey links with sun-dried tomatoes and basil, and the smoked duck and turkey sausages. The links cost $36.95, $37.95 and $38.95 respectively for five pounds (the minimum order). Shipping is extra; call 415-285-6660 to order.

SUPER CIDER

Apricot Apple Cider from Biringer Farm is perfect for cool-weather entertaining. Sip it on the rocks, sparkled with seltzer or spiked with rum. Or try the distinctive tastes of the apple ciders blended with strawberries or raspberries. All three flavors are available in 24-ounce bottles for $5.95 each, plus shipping. To order by telephone, dial 800-448-8212.

SWEET SPREAD

Vermont Maple Butter, a thick, creamy spread made from pure maple syrup, tastes terrific on everything from buckwheat pancakes to corn muffins to johnnycakes. A 22-ounce jar is $10.95, plus shipping, from The Vermont Country Store; telephone 802-362-2400 to order.

ORGANIC-BY-MAIL

If you'd like to prepare more meals with organically grown foods but don't know where to find them, several mail-order companies can help. For free catalogs, call Gold Mine Natural Food Co. at 800-475-FOOD or Fiddler's Green Farm at 207-338-3568. For a catalog offering organically grown herbs, send $1 to the Meadowbrook Herb Garden, P.O. Box 578, Fairfield, CT 06430.

NUTS FOR YOU

If you're planning a cocktail party, be sure to have plenty of spicy Cajun-Creole Hot Nuts on hand. Available from the folks at Mo Hotta-Mo Betta, the irresistible peanuts are sold in 16-ounce mesh bags for $4.75 each, plus

shipping. To order, call 800-462-3220 or write to P.O. Box 4136, San Luis Obispo, CA 93403.

THE REALLY BIG APPLE
Here's a truly sophisticated version of a kid-pleasing treat: The Apple by Attivo. This Bay Area confectionery double-dips Granny Smith apples into pure cream caramel and bittersweet chocolate. Enjoy them plain or with a coating of either fresh roasted macadamia nuts or crumbled cocoa *biscotti*. A sampler of three apples costs $27.50 and can be ordered by phoning 800-3-ATTIVO.

NEW YORK'S FINEST
Taste the sweet side of New York: Goodies from William Greenberg Jr. Desserts are available by mail. The Upper East Side bakery's best-seller? Schnecken, a spiral of sour cream pastry rolled up with raisins, pecans and cinnamon. And don't be shy about stocking up: The pastries freeze beautifully and can be reheated in the microwave. Choose from two sizes: large ($38 per dozen, $62.50 for two dozen) or a "baby" version ($25.50 per dozen, $39 for two dozen). To order, call toll free 800-255-8278.

HONEY OF A TOPPING
Raspberry Honey Creme makes a luscious, all-natural topping for toast, ice cream or yogurt. The spread (and the other honey-blend flavors of apricot, blueberry, blackberry and strawberry) is sold in two sizes: a 12-ounce jar for $5 and a 2¼-ounce sampler for $1.50, both plus shipping. To order, telephone Oregon Apiaries at 800-736-2781.

PLAN ON PASTA
Attenzione, all pasta lovers: Want a unique itinerary for your next trip to Italy? The Insider's Italy Travel Advisory is a consulting service perfect for planning any Italian vacation. For more information, contact John Goodrum, 264 North Whisman Road, Suite 9, Mountain View, CA 94043; 415-961-7441.

BEEF PLUS
Cured with Courvoisier and flavored with savory spices, this smoked beef tenderloin is the makings of a great sandwich. Delivered ready to eat, the two-pound boneless cut also makes a quick centerpiece for party buffets. It costs $59.95; from Cavanaugh Lakeview Farms, P.O. Box 580, Chelsea, MI 48118; 800-243-4438.

DIG THESE CHIPS
Delightful, crunchy Terra Chips, made from root vegetables, are positively addictive. Yam, yuca, taro, batata, parsnip, sweet potato, lotus root and celery root are thinly sliced, fried and lightly salted. All in all, a guaranteed conversation piece—serve with aperitifs or your favorite sandwiches. An eight-ounce bag costs $7.95 at Balducci's, 424 Avenue of the Americas, New York, NY 10011; telephone 212-673-2600.

BLUE-RIBBON CHEESE
The savory torta from Oregon's Rising Sun Farm is a sumptuous blend of cheese (including cream cheese, Parmesan and Romano) layered with minced dried tomatoes and pesto. Serve it with aperitifs or with salad as a cheese course. The torta also makes a terrific gift packed in a basket with loaves of crusty Italian bread and a bottle of wine. Three 8-ounce tortas are $30; six tortas, $45; twelve tortas, $84; all postage paid. To order, contact Rising Sun Farm, 5126 South Pacific Highway, Phoenix, OR 97535; 800-888-0795.

KLATCH THIS
Cool mornings are perfect for lingering over hot mugs of tea or coffee. Set out a Hungarian Coffee Cake from Sweet Things Bakery, and you've got an instant coffee klatch. The scrumptious sour cream cake, swirled with cocoa, brown sugar, cinnamon and walnuts, serves 12 to 14. It's $17.50, plus shipping. Call 415-388-8583 to order.

 *Books*

FRENCH STYLE

Pierre Deux's Paris Country (Clarkson Potter, 1991) is a handsome book celebrating the arts, antiques and traditions of Paris and its environs. It's also a regional guide to sight-seeing, dining and shopping, plus it includes a list of public gardens and parks, local festivals, fairs and weekly markets.

SOUTHERN TREASURE

Everything you need to know about great cooking southern style can be found in *Around the Southern Table* (Simon & Schuster, 1991). Filled with historical anecdotes, personal remembrances and two hundred delicious recipes, this book was written by *Bon Appétit* senior editor Sarah Belk.

Virginia-born but a New York convert, Belk now enjoys the best of both her worlds, although living in Manhattan has not been without its challenges. "The bagels here are great," she says, "but you've got to search high and low for a decent ham hock."

GOOD WINE READING

The Right Wine by Tom Maresca (Grove Weidenfeld, 1990) is a user-friendly guide for the novice as well as the serious oenophile. There are practical suggestions on "what to serve when" for everything from brunch (most people prefer white to red) to a cookout (pour "unthreatening" wines, like jug, simple domestic varietals or uncomplicated imports). The author also gives tips on ordering wine in a restaurant, plus how—and why—to cellar certain wines.

ITALIAN GOES AMERICAN

We Called It Macaroni by Nancy Verde Barr (Knopf, 1990) is a fascinating read about the heritage of southern Italian cooking in America. The author, who is of Italian ancestry, offers hundreds of simple, healthful recipes

that will tempt you into the kitchen. Historical information and anecdotes add to the fun.

FASTER FOOD

Two new microwave books help make meals a snap. The recipes in *Better by Microwave* by Lori Longbotham and Marie Simmons (Dutton, 1990) are tempting and easy to follow. Try their lemon-thyme poached eggs, tomato-ginger pasta sauce and scallop salad with cilantro-lime dressing.

In *Moghul Microwave: Cooking Indian Food the Modern Way* (William Morrow, 1990), author Julie Sahni presents classic Indian dishes microwave style—from fiery shrimp *vindaloo* to persimmon-plum chutney. She also discusses the basics for cooking lentils and rice, plus how to roast various spices for curry powder.

DELICIOUS ITALIAN HISTORY

The Heritage of Italian Cooking (Random House, 1990) by Lorenza de' Medici is a tempting collection of recipes that trace the evolution of Italian cuisine from the elaborate banquets of the Roman, Renaissance and Rococo eras to today's lighter style. The book's extraordinary art—reproductions of food-related paintings by noted Italian artists—makes it a visual feast as well.

TWO FOR DESSERT

Sweet Times: Simple Desserts for Every Occasion (William Morrow and Company, 1991) by Dorie Greenspan offers easy-to-make treats, from kids' cookies to a suave, frozen honey-yogurt mousse. Dessert lovers will also want to snap up another recent cookbook from William Morrow: Flo Braker's *Sweet Miniatures: The Art of Making Bite-Size Desserts* (1991).

🍎 *Restaurants & People*

DALLAS CHIC

Overlooking a beautiful garden, the newly opened Conservatory at the Hotel Crescent Court in Dallas has quickly become an "occasion" restaurant. The inspired menu features new American classics, like lobster corn soup and warm peach tart with Brazil nut ice cream. (The Conservatory, Hotel Crescent Court, 400 Crescent Court, Dallas, TX 75201; 214-871-3242.)

ROOM WITH A VIEW

La Maison Blanche-15 Montaigne is one of the hottest new dining spots in Paris and a stunning tribute to its founder, the late two-star chef José Lampreia. Perched atop the Champs-Elysées Theater on the avenue Montaigne, it has an incredible view of the city. Chef José Martinez is forging his own culinary style while continuing to offer many of the unique dishes that made Lampreia famous (15 avenue Montaigne, 75008 Paris; 47-23-55-99).

HONG KONG WINNER

Hong Kong probably has more restaurants per square mile than any other place on earth, which makes deciding where to go for dinner quite difficult, especially for the first-time visitor. But we have just the place. Lai Ching Heen is The Regent hotel's luxuriously appointed Chinese restaurant, and it's one of the city's best. The incredible food of chef Cheung Kam Chuen is matched by an equally incredible view of Victoria Harbor. (Lai Ching Heen, The Regent, Salisbury Road, Tsimshatsui, Kowloon; 721-1211.)

PRIDE OF NEW YORK

Turback's, in the heart of New York's scenic Finger Lakes region, is *the* restaurant for sampling the best of the Empire State. Housed in an 1852 gingerbread Victorian mansion in Ithaca,

Turback's features an array of great dishes, and most of the ingredients—even the fist-size heads of garlic—come from nearby farms. Specialties include spicy cured salmon, Catskill Mountain smoked duck, and meat loaf made from buffalo raised in the state. There's also a fine selection of New York wines. (Turback's, 919 Elmira Rd., Ithaca, NY 14850; 607-272-6484.)

HOT 'LANTA

Atlanta may be the heart of the Deep South (home of fried chicken and corn bread), but it's also the place for some of the best Italian food in the country. Veni, Vidi, Vici is the city's hottest new restaurant. Pastas are authentic and homemade; soups are bold and full flavored. And don't miss the risottos—they're the perfect comfort food. The stylish, postmodern setting makes this a delightful urban retreat. (Veni, Vidi, Vici, 41 14th Street, Atlanta, GA 30309; 404-875-8424.)

FLORIDA: NEW CUBAN COOKING

Flying south for winter? Planning a vacation in the sun? Yuca restaurant in Coral Gables is not to be missed, according to our Florida taste bud, Steven Raichlen. Their "new Cuban" cuisine is deliciously innovative. (Yuca, 177 Giralda, Coral Gables, FL 33134; telephone 305-444-4448.)

A HAWAIIAN LEGEND

Hawaii superchef Roy Yamaguchi, chef-owner of the long-popular Roy's in Honolulu, will open a new restaurant, Roy's Park Bistro, in Waikiki this spring. And that's not all: His Kahana Bar and Grill opened on Maui in December.

ON THE MARK

Chocoholics take note: Look no further than The Mark hotel in Manhattan for the dessert of your dreams. Chocolate Gourmandises pairs a warm, rich, fudgelike cake (glazed with more chocolate and topped with gold leaf) with a chocolate cookie cup filled with vanilla ice cream. It's a sublime ending to the dining room's equally sublime appetizers and main courses. For reservations, telephone 212-879-1864.

RETURN OF THE RED CAR

Back before Los Angeles became a parking lot, the city's inhabitants moved around town on a remarkably efficient rail system known locally as the Red Cars. The recently opened Red Car Grill in West Hollywood is a stunning mahogany and marble remembrance of that bygone era. Prominent restaurant designer Pat Kuleto has filled the space with period touches that give it the feel of an early California railway station. Owned by the same people who launched the successful Engine Co. No. 28 restaurant downtown, the new spot features a varied, uncomplicated menu, including dry-aged New York steak and grilled calf's liver. (Red Car Grill, 8571 Santa Monica Boulevard, West Hollywood, CA 90069; 213-652-9263.)

SEATTLE, ITALIAN-STYLE

Saleh Joudeh started professional life as a doctor. Now he's a chef. And his restaurant Saleh al Lago, on the shore of Green Lake, has become one of Seattle's favorite Italian eateries. The pastel-colored dining room is casual and airy, with a view of the open kitchen, display cases full of meats and a smattering of bottles from the formidable list of Italian and domestic wines. The menu is friendly and inviting. (Saleh al Lago Ristorante e Bar, 6804 Greenlake Way North, Seattle, WA 98115; 206-524-4044.)

ARIZONA LIGHT

Top of the Rock, the elegant dining spot at The Buttes, has created a new leaner, lighter menu. The resort restaurant's southwestern-accented cuisine now includes more vegetable-based sauces, as well as dishes using less butter and cream and more herbs and peppers. With such offerings on the menu as crab croissant pizza, cherry duck breast and honey-seared rack of lamb filled with feta cheese, spinach and garlic, there are lots of reasons to be "light"-headed while dining in this elevated room with a view. (Top of the Rock, The Buttes, 2000 Westcourt Way, Tempe, AZ 85282; 602-225-9000, ext. 5070.)

TEA AND TRANQUILLITY

Next time you're in the San Francisco Bay Area, treat yourself to a bit of Japanese-inspired tranquillity at the thoroughly unique O Chamé in Berkeley. Chef-owner David Vardy, who is responsible for this lovely restaurant, spent several years in Japan studying tea ceremony and the foods that are part of it. His experience shows itself in everything from the warm interior, with its Brazilian wood and etched pale orange plaster walls, to the exquisitely prepared and presented food. (O Chamé Restaurant and Tea Room, 1830 Fourth Street, Berkeley, CA 94710; 415-841-8783.)

EATING TUSCAN IN L.A.

Although Los Angeles has no shortage of places serving terrific northern Italian dishes, some key components of this popular cuisine don't get much attention. Foods like rabbit, squab, sweetbreads and tripe might seem exotic, but they are dietary staples in Italy's famous Tuscany region. And Olí Olá serves them with pride. Executive chef Agostino Sciandri has teamed with partners Kathie and Michael Gordon to create a trattoria in Pacific Palisades that is authentic to the core, with terra-cotta tiles, brick walls and a wonderfully hearty menu of dishes that pay honest homage to their Tuscan origins. (Olí Olá, 15200 Sunset Boulevard, Pacific Palisades, CA 90272; 213-459-9214.)

❦ *Getaways*

SPACE-AGE HOTEL

Located in the heart of St.-Germain-des-Prés at 29 rue Jacob, the intimate La Villa hotel has become the favorite Paris base of travelers from the worlds of fashion and photography. The Jetsons would feel right at home here—the rooms are outfitted with brightly colored space-age furniture and light fixtures. Comfort is never sacrificed for style, however, and the staff is attentive—and bilingual. Another bonus: A bar and jazz club are located on the two lower levels. For hotel reservations, call 43-26-60-00.

VIVA MEXICO!

Culinary "Journeys in Taste" to Mexico, guided by cookbook author Patricia Quintana, include hands-on cooking workshops plus visits to local restaurants, markets and sites of historical interest. For information, call Holiday Travels, 800-553-7982 or 918-584-5821. Before you go, pick up Michelin's green guide to Mexico (English language) for good information about archaeological sites and the Mexican culture.

MUNICH TREASURE

The new Hotel Rafael in Munich is so grand—replete with sweeping staircases and priceless antiques—that it's hard to believe there are only 74 rooms and suites. No two are alike, yet each boasts unparalleled luxury, from butler and chambermaid call buttons to Porthault linens and robes, down comforters, marble baths, VCRs and telefax outlets. In the dining room, the hotel showcases the skills of Frank Heppner, who incorporates the flavors of the Orient into his contemporary European cooking. Try the curried langoustines with lemongrass noodles or guinea hen on a ragout of morels. Later, you can work off the calories in the rooftop swimming pool. (Hotel Rafael, Neuturmstrasse 1, 8000 Munich 2, Germany; 089.29.09.80 or, in the U.S., 800-223-1588.)

TENNESSEE WALTZ

The Smoky Mountains boast magnificent scenery all year 'round. Take in the sights with a long hike while staying at the Blackberry Farm inn in eastern Tennessee. The charming, 1,100-acre retreat (with 25 antique-filled guest rooms) is worth a detour, indeed. For information, contact Blackberry Farm, 1471 West Millers Cove Road, Walland, TN 37886; 615-984-8166.

ISLAND RETREAT

Need a great getaway? The Cotton Bay Club on Eleuthera in the Bahamas is our new favorite. With 70 rooms, the resort is big enough to offer all the amenities, yet small enough to give guests that away-from-it-all feeling. Call 800-334-3523 or 809-334-6156 for information and reservations.

GREAT ESCAPE

Get the keys to a charming Italian villa or French farmhouse through Bowhills. Their new brochure has details on scores of rentals; it's an indispensable guide for planning a unique European vacation. To order the $12 catalog, call 800-438-4748 or, in Los Angeles, 310-247-8612.

EUROPE IN UTAH

An old-world feeling pervades the recently renovated Inn at Temple Square in Salt Lake City, from the wrought-iron front gate and cobblestone courtyard to the wainscoted Edwardian-style interior to the traditionally costumed housekeepers in black dresses and ruffled white pinafore aprons. Accommodations include such niceties as free morning newspaper, terry-cloth robes and Crabtree & Evelyn cosmetics packages. And there's the Carriage Court Restaurant for especially satisfying complimentary breakfasts. (The Inn at Temple Square, 71 West South Temple, Salt Lake City, UT 84101; 800-843-4668.)

NEW MEXICO FIND

The Inn of the Anasazi, named for the native Americans who originally inhabited the site it occupies, is a unique addition to the Santa Fe hotel scene. It's located across from the Palace of the Governors, the oldest public building in the United States, amid the pueblo-style structures of the town's historic Plaza District. The 59 rooms and suites are furnished with the work of local artisans, and each has a traditional kiva fireplace. In the dining room, organic meats and vegetables from local farmers star in chef Peter Zimmer's daily-changing menu, a creative blending of Native American, northern New Mexico and American cowboy cooking. (Inn of the Anasazi, 113 Washington Avenue, Santa Fe, NM 87501; 505-988-3030.)

GOING ITALIAN IN SONOMA

The view of the rolling hills across from the rustic Italian villa is accented with vineyards and old farms, but don't think Tuscany—think Sonoma County. The Kenwood Inn—complete with Italian-style grape arbor, fountain and pool—has four comfortable, well-appointed guest rooms that are just about the most romantic thing going in this section of the Valley of the Moon. And don't miss the sumptuous breakfasts prepared by innkeepers Terry and Roseann Grimm. (Kenwood Inn, 10400 Sonoma Hwy., Kenwood, CA 95452; 707-833-1293.)

MOUNTAIN CLASSIC

Located in the heart of Durango, Colorado's, historic district, the four-story, red-brick Strater Hotel is a Victorian beauty from top to bottom. Its 93 guest rooms are furnished with one of the world's finest collections of American Victorian walnut antiques. The Victorian era meets the Wild West at the hotel's Diamond Belle Saloon, and certified Angus beef from Colorado stars on the dinner menu of the hotel's restaurant, called Henry's. (The Strater Hotel, P.O. Drawer E, Durango, CO 81302; 800-247-4431 or, in Colorado, 303-247-4431.)

For the Kitchen & Table

COOKING GOOD

Newlyweds stocking their first kitchen will delight in T-Fal's "Paris" cookware line. The exterior is coated with white-porcelain enamel, so the cookware is resistant to scratches and stains and is dishwasher-safe. Nonstick surfaces and steam-vented covers add to the versatility. Sold separately or in an eight-piece set (about $149), it's available at department and specialty stores nationwide. Telephone 201-575-1060 for a store near you.

A MONET TO GROW

Most flower lovers agree that the best centerpieces are those you create yourself. And what could be more appealing than one made with an array of flowers straight out of an impressionist painting? The lush, luminous canvases of Claude Monet have inspired a seed collection called the Flowers of Monet. From White Swan Ltd., this palette of over 60 varieties includes poppies, cornflowers, blue flax and foxglove. At specialty stores nationwide, it costs about $30. Call 800-233-7926 for a store in your area.

SITTING PRETTY

Stackable chairs are a blessing for those who entertain a lot but don't like to bother with rentals. The shapely specimen, called "Rio" by its designer, Pascal Mourgue, has a seat and back of stained ash, with lacquered metal legs. Of course, chairs this stylish make a good impression all by themselves—move them out to the porch to complete a contemporary setting. They cost $199 each and can be found at the Modernage boutique, 795 Broadway, New York, NY 10003; telephone 212-674-5603.

GARDEN FRESH

The new "Maria Paradies" dishware pattern from Rosenthal's Classic Rose collection combines the softness of flowers and fruits with a clean, stylish design. A five-piece place setting costs about $98. It's available at department stores and specialty shops nationwide; telephone 718-417-3400 for locations.

CUTTING EDGE

Wüsthof Trident has introduced a new cutlery collection called Grand Prix. Each knife in the 5-piece set combines a strong, sharp blade with a sturdy bolster for safety, balance and comfort. The newly designed handle is slip resistant. The eight-inch chef's knife—a favorite of most every cook—is available for $80 at Williams-Sonoma and other specialty stores nationwide. For the store nearest you, telephone 914-347-2185.

COUNTRY CHIC

Thomasville's new furniture line, called "Country Inns and Back Roads," is an inspired collection of reproductions patterned after pieces found in some of America's most popular country inns. The collection consists of two categories: "American Parlor" comprises formal, mahogany furniture; "Country Cottage" includes rustic oak pieces that have been burnished and either antiqued or painted, including a nineteenth-century-style Gathering Table (about $2,240) that measures 40 by 68 by 30 inches and comes with two 20-inch-wide leaves. For a store near you, call 800-225-0265.

COOL BLUES

A terrific set of cobalt blue "New England" glasses can add instant pizzazz to the table. They're just the right size (ten-ounce capacity) for serving everything from seltzer to iced tea to highballs. A set of four five-inch-tall water glasses (order no. 50267) or four-inch-tall tumblers (order no. 50265) is $38, plus shipping. Contact The Museum of Fine Arts, Boston, Catalog Sales, P.O. Box 1044, Boston, MA 02120; telephone 800-225-5592.

NOT RUN-OF-THE-MILL

A trio of shapely pepper mills designed by Marco Magni can grace even the most elegant table. Inspired by minarets, mosques and mythical domes, these grinders are made of silver plate and sleek polished wood. The ebony is $180; mahogany, $170; beech, $155. They're at the LS Collection, 765 Madison Avenue, New York, NY 10021; telephone 212-472-3355.

THE WRIGHT SETTING

Just like his architectural designs, Frank Lloyd Wright's tableware is bold, elegant and blends with a variety of other styles. Wright's "Imperial" pattern—designed in 1922 for the Imperial Hotel in Tokyo—was recently introduced by Tiffany & Co. This dinnerware joins their exclusive collection of crystal, silver and porcelain designed by the inimitable architect. The five-piece place setting is $210 at Tiffany & Co. stores.

HOT STUFF

Danish architect Knud Holscher designed a stylish, sturdy thermos that combines modern form and function perfectly. The stainless steel beauty is $150 from Georg Jensen. Want one? Contact Royal Copenhagen at 914-428-8222 for a store near you.

HEAVY-DUTY LIGHTWEIGHT

The nonstick surface on Farberware's new Millennium line of stainless steel cookware is virtually indestructible: It's dishwasher safe, metal utensils can't scratch it and it's guaranteed to last for 20 years. The line is available in open-stock pieces as well as seven-, eight- and ten-piece sets in department stores or by mail (call 800-327-2379).

🍎 *Diet News*

STATE OF THE NATION

Are most Americans fit? Not according to recent findings by the U.S. Public Health Service. So helping us be just that is the focus of *Healthy Living for Life,* an informative booklet from Weight Watchers and the National Center for Nutrition and Dietetics. The guide—which is part of a national health drive called Healthy People 2000—offers practical tips on ways to eat better, improve fitness, maintain proper weight and make positive lifestyle changes. A short quiz enables readers to put together their own health profile. For the free booklet, write to *Healthy Living for Life,* Weight Watchers, P.O. Box 4383, Syosset, NY 11775.

GO FOR THE JUICE

Tufts University reports that many Americans aren't getting enough calcium, according to the USDA's National Food Consumption Survey. In fact, nearly seven out of ten people polled are getting less than half the recommended daily amount. The suggested intake is three servings of calcium-rich foods totalling eight hundred milligrams a day.

So how can you get all the calcium your body needs? Milk may be the traditional choice, but a convenient new source is calcium-fortified orange juice. Nutritionists have found that one brand in particular, Citrus Hill Plus Calcium, provides a highly absorbent type of calcium called CCM (calcium combined with citric and malic acids, two naturally occurring fruit acids). One six-ounce glass of this orange juice provides 225 milligrams of calcium. Reason enough to switch from coffee to juice at break time.

FROM THE HEART

In a land that's famous for buttery croissants, creamy sauces and fatty foie gras, how can a healthy heart prevail? Scientists have been pondering this paradox ever since a study by the World Health Organization revealed that, of 18 industrialized Western countries, France has the lowest death rate from heart disease. In fact, a middle-aged man in the United States is more than twice as likely to have a heart attack as his French counterpart.

Attempting to unravel the mystery of the healthy French heart, researchers in France and elsewhere are investigating nutritional factors that may set the French apart. Under closest scrutiny so far: more consumption of fruit, vegetables, bread and particularly wine. On average, the French drink three glasses of *vin* a day—far more than other nationalities.

LESS THAN FRUITFUL

As more Americans monitor their intake of fat and cholesterol, two important food groups are being overlooked. Pollsters sponsored by the American Dietetic Association and the International Food Information Council asked consumers what healthful changes they were making in their diets. Of those polled, 48 percent take more vitamins, 64 percent eat more fiber and 24 percent use more olive oil. But only 6 percent consume more vegetables, fruits and fruit juices. These results were published in the *Tufts University Diet & Nutrition Letter.* Experts at the USDA recommend three to five daily servings of vegetables and two to four of fruit.

DIALING FOR RELIEF

If you're one of the nearly 30 million Americans who suffer from food allergies, around-the-clock advice is now a phone call away. The Food Allergy Center operates a toll-free line that provides useful information pertaining to adverse food reactions and their treatment. Dial 800-YES-RELIEF.

ORGANIC BEEF

Coleman natural meats was the nation's first producer of organic and natural beef, and today it's the largest. Recently, the Colorado-based company became the first U.S. beef producer to receive certification from the Organic Crop Improvement Association. Coleman's natural and organic beef cattle are raised without antibiotics or growth hormones; the organic beef cattle also get feed that is certified to be free of synthetic fertilizers, herbicides and pesticides. Look for their natural beef in natural foods stores and specialty foods stores nationwide; find the organic beef in select supermarkets in Boston, Houston, Oklahoma City and Denver.

EGG SAFETY

The care and handling of eggs are the topics of a new booklet from the American Egg Board. Presented in an informative Q&A format, it covers many concerns expressed by consumers, including the use of room-temperature eggs in recipes and ways to reduce the possibility of bacterial contamination in dishes calling for raw eggs. *The Egg Handling & Care Guide* is available by sending an S.A.S.E. (business size) to The Incredible Edible Egg Number 33, P.O. Box 733, Park Ridge, IL 60068.

SWEETS GO LIGHT

Sara Lee's new line of Free & Light baked goods offers dieters guilt-free desserts and morning treats. (We especially like the apple Danish and cherry streusel pie.) These versions of longtime favorites, including chocolate cake and pound cake, have one third the calories, less sodium, no cholesterol and are 98 percent fat-free. What's more, they contain no artificial sweeteners, artificial flavors, tropical oils or preservatives.

COOKING WITH COCOA

Pure, all natural, cholesterol-free cocoa powder is the featured ingredient in Hershey's new *Light & Luscious Chocolate Desserts* brochure. Unsweetened cocoa powder is the only chocolate baking ingredient approved by the American Heart Association for use in fat-restricted diets. Cooking tips and nutritional information accompany receipes—try the chocolate ricotta cheesecake with just 160 calories per serving. For a free copy, send a self-addressed, business-size stamped envelope to "Light & Luscious," 40 West 57th Street, Suite 1400, New York, NY 10019.

DANISH IMPORT

Diet cheeses often rank low in the taste department, but we found MD Light's new Havarti cheese full bodied and surprisingly flavorful. Best of all, it's lower in cholesterol and has 33 percent fewer calories and 40 percent less fat than regular Havarti. Look for this smooth, mild Danish cheese at supermarkets and specialty foods stores nationwide. It costs $5.25 per pound.

WHEAT-FREE RECIPES

A new book, with over two hundred recipes, offers delicious relief for anyone who is allergic to wheat. *The Gluten-free Gourmet: Living Well Without Wheat* (Henry Holt and Company, 1990) by Bette Hagman presents creative recipes for celiacs—people allergic to the gluten found in wheat, oats, barley and rye. The author specializes in developing healthy versions of foods that are typically off limits, like pizza, pasta and baked goods. Tasty gluten-free recipes range from three-cheese lasagne to banana cream pie to chunky chocolate squares. The book also supplies a list of mail-order food companies carrying different gluten-free products.

🍒 Credits and Acknowledgments

The following people and restaurants contributed the recipes included in this book:

A Sousceyrac, Paris, France
Actuelle, Dallas, Texas
Albuquerque Hilton Hotel, Albuquerque, New Mexico
Margo Alofsin
Margot Andrew
Apicius, Paris, France
Au Cochon d'Or, Paris, France
Azur, Minneapolis, Minnesota
Mary Baker
Leah M. Balk
Melanie Barnard
Beekman Arms, Rhinebeck, New York
Sarah Belk
The Berkeley, London, England
Biba, Boston, Massachusetts
James and Sidney Bonnet
Charleen Borger
Blair Box
Caledonian Hotel, Edinburgh, Scotland
Jonna Veitch Carls
Carnegie Deli of Beverly Hills, Los Angeles, California
Roxanne E. Chan
Judy Collins
Gina and Courtney Conte
Copper Beech Inn, Ivoryton, Connecticut
Lane S. Crowther
The Culinary Institute of America, Hyde Park, New York
Cunard Line
The Dakota Restaurant, Covington, Louisiana
Natalie Danford
Brooke Dojny
Duck Club Restaurant, Lafayette Park Hotel, Lafayette, California

Sydney A. Ducker
George's at the Cove, La Jolla, California
Terry Gibraltar
Glen Ellen Winery, Glen Ellen, California
Greens at Fort Mason, San Francisco, California
Lynn Hagee
Ellen Hallal
Lynne and Howard Halpern
Holland House Inn, Victoria, British Columbia
The House of Seafood, Lihue, Hawaii
Jules Verne, Paris, France
Karen Kaplan
Kathleen's Fantastic Food & Catering, Newport, Rhode Island
Jeanne Thiel Kelley
Susan and Larry Kessler
Kiawah Island Resort and Villas, Charleston, South Carolina
Kristine Kidd
Elinor Klivans
JoAnn and David Krajeski
La Creme de La Creme, Oakland, California
Lark Creek Inn, Larkspur, California
Les Auteurs, Royal Oak, Michigan
Jan and Basil Liascos
Anna Meshkat Liebling
Abby Mandel
Michael McLaughlin
Mirassou Vineyards, San Jose, California
Selma Brown Morrow
Joanie Moscoe
Moustache Cafe, Los Angeles, California
Olde Port Inn, Avila Beach, California
Joe Ortiz
O'Shea's Ltd., Tacoma, Washington

Oyster Bar & Restaurant, New York, New York
The Palace, The Cincinnatian Hotel, Cincinnati, Ohio
The Pavilion Restaurant, Port Townsend, Washington
Portobello Yacht Club, Pleasure Island, Walt Disney Resort, Orlando, Florida
Tammy Randerman
Rebecca and Ralph Riskin
The Ritz-Carlton, Buckhead, Atlanta, Georgia
Carole Rodkey
Romanoff, Hamilton, Bermuda
Roy's Restaurant, Honolulu, Hawaii
San Domenico, New York, New York
Richard Sax
Michele Sbrana
Gina Schild
Lana Sills
Marie Simmons
The Sugar Mill Restaurant-Rotisserie, Half Moon Golf, Tennis & Beach Club, Montego Bay, Jamaica
Sarah Tenaglia
Tarla Thiel
Dodie Thompson
Timothy's Bar & Restaurant, Louisville, Kentucky
Trattoria Mitchelli, Seattle, Washington
Ann Ferguson Ward
Cynthia Paige Ward
Wheatleigh, Lenox, Massachusetts
Julie Wilson
Paula Zsiray

"News '91" text supplied by James Badham, Sarah Belk, Barbara Fairchild, Vene Franco, Ruth Gardner-Low, Janice Wald Henderson, Ken Hom, Sally Nirenberg, Steven Raichlen

Foreword and chapter introductions written by Laurie Glenn Buckle

Editorial Staff:
William J. Garry
Barbara Fairchild
Laurie Glenn Buckle

Copy Editor:
Marilyn Novell

Rights and Permissions:
Gaylen Ducker Grody
Katherine O'Kennedy

Graphics Staff:
Bernard Rotondo
Sandy Douglas

Production:
Joan Valentine

Indexer:
Barbara Wurf

The Knapp Press
is a wholly owned subsidiary of
KNAPP COMMUNICATIONS CORPORATION

Composition by Andresen Typographics, Tucson, Arizona

This book is set in Sabon, a face designed by Jan Teischold in 1967 and based on early fonts engraved by Garamond and Granjon.